GARBAGE

FOLLOW THE PATH OF YOUR TRASH

WITH ENVIRONMENTAL SCIENCE ACTIVITIES FOR KIDS

Donna Latham
Illustrated by Tom Casteel

Titles in the **Environmental Science** book set

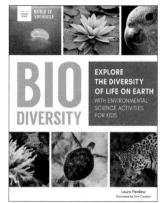
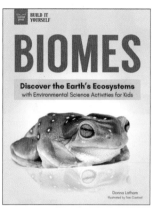

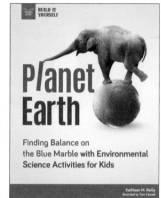

Check out more titles at www.nomadpress.net

Nomad Press
A division of Nomad Communications
10 9 8 7 6 5 4 3 2 1

This book was manufactured by CGB Printers,
North Mankato, Minnesota, United States
March 2019, Job #265268

ISBN Softcover: 978-1-61930-747-6
ISBN Hardcover: 978-1-61930-744-5

Educational Consultant, Marla Conn

Questions regarding the ordering of this book should be addressed to
Nomad Press
2456 Christian St.
White River Junction, VT 05001
www.nomadpress.net

Contents

Interested in Primary Sources?

Look for this icon. Use a smartphone or tablet app to scan the QR code and explore more! Photos are also primary sources because a photograph takes a picture at the moment something happens.

 You can find a list of URLs on the Resources page. If the QR code doesn't work, try searching the internet with the Keyword Prompts to find other helpful sources.

🔎 garbage

How Long Is It Around?

You might think that aluminum soda can is simply gone once you've tossed it in the trash, but guess what? That can is going to be around for a long, long time. Take a look! In the chart below, one trash can represents 20 years.

🗑 = 20 years

Glass bottle	1 million years	🗑🗑🗑🗑🗑🗑🗑🗑
Monofilament fishing line	600 years	🗑🗑🗑🗑🗑🗑🗑🗑
Plastic beverage bottles	450 years	🗑🗑🗑🗑🗑🗑🗑🗑
Disposable diapers	450 years	🗑🗑🗑🗑🗑🗑🗑🗑
Foamed plastic buoy	80 years	🗑🗑🗑🗑
Foamed plastic cups	50 years	🗑🗑🗑
Tin cans	50 years	🗑🗑🗑
Nylon fabric	30–40 years	🗑🗑
Plastic bag	10–20 years	🗑
Cigarette butt	1–5 years	🗑
Plywood	1–3 years	🗑
Waxed milk carton	3 months	🗑
Apple core	2 months	🗑
Newspaper	6 weeks	🗑
Orange or banana peel	2–5 weeks	🗑

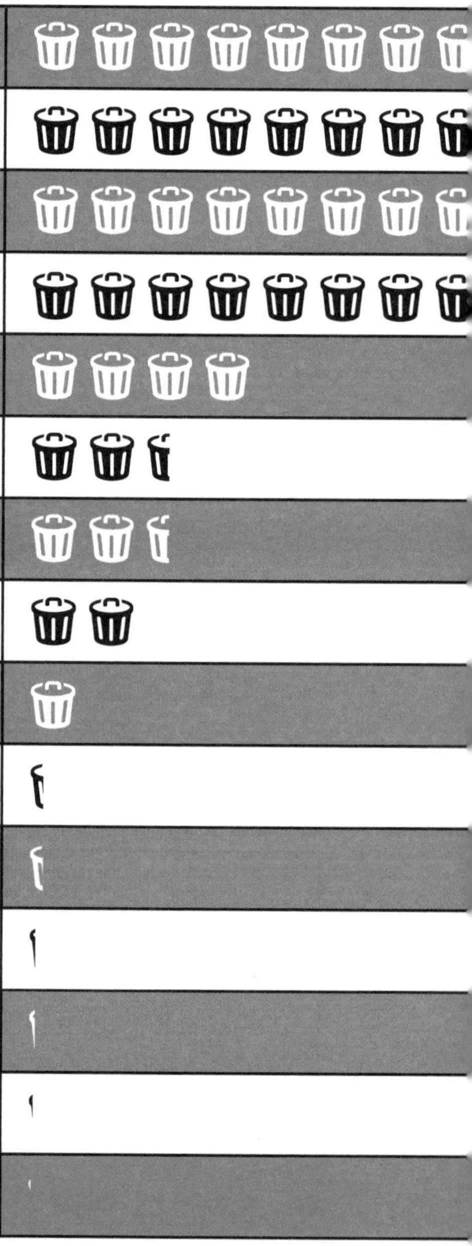

HOW LONG IS IT AROUND?

Imagine these continuing for
more than four football fields!

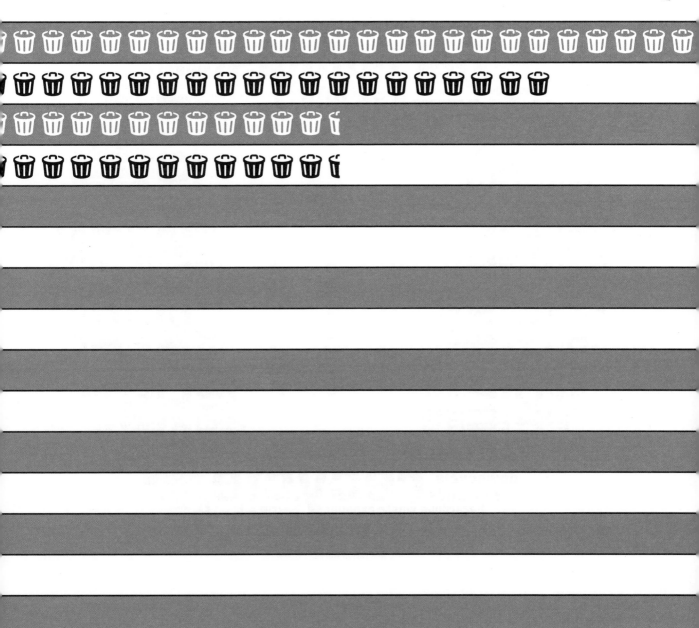

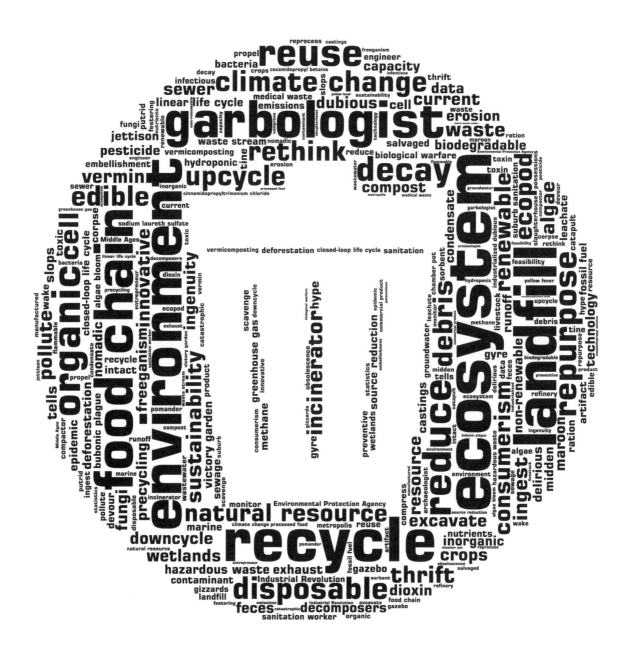

A THROWAWAY
WORLD

What have you tossed in the trash today? A gnawed apple core? A mangled plastic straw? Maybe you threw away a tattered backpack or an old pair of sneakers.

Trash is stuff we consider useless. Another word for trash is garbage. We throw garbage "away." Anywhere you find people, you'll find garbage—mounds and mounds of it. A **gyre** of plastic trash floats in the middle of the ocean. Garbage is even **marooned** on the surface of the moon.

ESSENTIAL QUESTION

Why does it matter where our garbage goes after we throw it out?

Usually, we don't realize how much stuff we throw away. In just one year, an average family of four in the United States churns out 6,351 pounds of **waste**. That's enough to fill a three-bedroom house to the ceiling.

1

WORDS TO KNOW

gyre: a spiral.

maroon: to leave someone or something trapped somewhere that's hard to get to.

waste: material that is not wanted.

landfill: a huge area of land where trash gets buried.

incinerator: a large furnace that burns trash.

wake: a trail of something left behind.

scavenge: to find usable bits and parts from discarded stuff.

After you throw away that empty potato chip bag, what happens? Do you lug your trash cans out to the curb at night, only to find them empty in the morning? Do you chuck your trash bags into the dumpster behind your building or at the dump, never to see them again? It's easy to get rid of garbage so you never have to see it again. Trash is out of sight, out of mind.

But—what happens to all that garbage once it leaves our hands?

Trash gets jam-packed into **landfills** or burned in **incinerators**. But trash doesn't always make it to a garbage can. It's often left behind as messy litter that people carelessly scatter in their **wake**. Litter flutters across our streets, parks, and beaches. No wonder so many people talk trash these days!

Beachfront garbage
credit: epSos.de (CC BY 2.0)

2

Bootprint on the moon

Garbage can even be found out of this world! During the historic 1969 *Apollo 11* mission, astronauts Neil Armstrong and Buzz Aldrin gathered rocks and soil from the surface of the moon. The astronauts left behind an American flag and a heap of space trash.

To lighten their spacecraft's load and make room to transport samples back to Earth, astronauts left empty food sacks, vomit bags, a TV camera, collection tongs, and magazines on the moon. They even left the space boots that made those famous footprints on the moon's surface.

About the Projects

Use projects and activities in this book to make your own discoveries about garbage and spark new ideas about ways to tackle waste. Don't have the suggested materials and supplies needed for a project? Think of items you can substitute. **Scavenge** stuff from a friend. Trade with someone. Of course, safety's first, so ask adults for help when handling sharp items and glue guns or when using the stove.

WORDS TO KNOW

reduce: to use less of something.

reuse: instead of tossing out an item, using it again or for a new or creative purpose.

recycle: shredding, squashing, pulping, or melting items to use the materials to create new products.

rethink: to reconsider—to think about something again and change your mind about it.

resource: things found in nature, such as wood or gold, that people can use.

debris: the scattered pieces of something that has been broken or destroyed.

THE FOUR Rs: REDUCE, REUSE, RECYCLE, RETHINK

In this book, you'll explore ways you can **reduce**, **reuse**, and **recycle** garbage. You'll also find ways to **rethink** choices you make every day. To reduce is to use less of a product or material so there's less waste. For example, instead of grabbing three paper towels to dry your hands after washing up, use one.

To reuse is to save things that you would normally throw out—and use them again or for another purpose. Turn an old beach towel into a cozy blanket for your pet. Pass along clothes to family or friends. Donate books to a library or shelter.

Rubbish Warriors

On your mark, get set, go! In 2018, a Swedish fitness craze washed ashore in the United States. Plogging! The word is a combination of the Swedish *plocka app*, which means "pick up," and the English word *jogging*. How does it work? Armed with gloves, garbage bags, and running shoes, joggers head out for trash runs. Along city streets, nature trails, and waterfronts, they scoop up plastic bottles, squashed cans, cigarette butts, and even dirty diapers. They recycle what they can and properly dispose of the rest. You try it! Go out for a plog! Take care of your body while you take care of the planet. In this book, you'll read about many Rubbish Warriors who decided to make a difference by tackling the garbage problems they see in the world. What can you do?

To recycle means to break down old items in order to make new ones. Recycling saves **resources** and energy. Some materials commonly recycled include plastic, paper, glass, and metal.

Definitions of Debris

There are lots of words to describe things we throw out. What does **debris** mean to you? You might imagine demolished walls left after a tornado whirls through a neighborhood. How about leftovers? Those are uneaten foods from last night's meal. What do the following terms for trash make you think of?

- bits and pieces
- cast-offs
- debris
- discards
- garbage
- junk
- leftovers
- litter
- odds and ends
- refuse
- rejects
- rubbish
- scraps
- surplus
- waste

WORDS TO KNOW

Environmental Protection Agency (EPA): a department of the U.S. government concerned with the environment and its impact on human health.

hazardous waste: a waste with properties that make it dangerous or capable of having a harmful effect on human health or the environment.

environment: everything in nature, living and nonliving, including animals, plants, rocks, soil, and water.

Rethinking is another crucial activity in the struggle against garbage. Rethinking means looking more closely at something and thinking again about your choices. By examining your habits, you might change them for the better.

For example, do you drink bottled water at soccer practice or dance rehearsal? Did you know it requires 1.5 million barrels of oil to produce a year's worth of bottled water? That's enough fuel for 100,000 cars for a year. After rethinking, you might fill a reusable stainless-steel water bottle instead.

In our throwaway world, we toss out trash constantly. But what does "out" really mean? And where, exactly, is "away?" What happens when we run out of "out" and "away?" Trash might be out of sight, but try to keep it in mind.

DID YOU KNOW?

Nail polish. Rat poison. Oven cleaner. According to the U.S. **Environmental Protection Agency (EPA)**, an average family produces 20 pounds of such **hazardous wastes** yearly.

Garbage Goals!

Kamikatsu, Japan, population 1,482, is dubbed "The Zero Waste Town." Dedicated stewards of the planet, people in Kamikatsu divide garbage into 34 recycling categories. The amazing result? They produce virtually no trash!

Watch a video to learn how Kamikatsu achieved this enormous, inspirational accomplishment. How might a program like this operate in your own community?

🔎 Stories town no trash

Like many people, you probably care about keeping the **environment** clean and healthy. In a world crowded with nearly 8 billion people, it's easy to think one person can't make a difference. But you can. Every effort counts. Become a rubbish warrior like the people you'll meet in this book!

Ready to take a hard look at the stuff we throw away? Let's follow the path of your trash!

Good Science Practices

Every good scientist keeps a science journal!

Scientists use the scientific method to keep their experiments organized. Choose a notebook to use as your science journal. As you read through this book and do the activities, keep track of your observations and record each step in a scientific method worksheet, like the one shown here.

Question: What are we trying to find out? What problem are we trying to solve?
Research: What is already known about the problem?
Hypothesis/Prediction: What do we think the answer will be?
Equipment: What supplies are we using?
Method: What procedure are we following?
Results: What happened? Why?

Each chapter of this book begins with an essential question to help guide your exploration of garbage and the environment. Keep the question in your mind as you read the chapter. At the end of each chapter, use your science journal to record your thoughts and answers.

ESSENTIAL QUESTION

Why does it matter where our garbage goes after we throw it out?

Chapter 1

HOW MUCH GARBAGE DO
YOU PRODUCE?

Families throw out old smartphones, laptops, avocado pits, blobs of burritos, and chicken bones. People dump ratty sweaters and raggedy blue jeans. We discard piles and piles of single-use **disposable** products, such as diapers, napkins, straws, and paper towels. Garbage is an unavoidable part of our lives.

In our throwaway world, we've racked up mind-boggling **statistics**. The United States alone generates a whopping 260 million tons of garbage a year. Enough trash to cover the giant state of Texas. Twice!

ESSENTIAL QUESTION

Do you produce more **inorganic** or **organic** waste?

From this gigantic amount, let's zoom in on just one person—you. If you're similar to the average American, then you produce about 4½ pounds of rubbish a day, more than 31 pounds a week. That's 1,638 pounds of trash a year!

What's rotting in those mounds of rubbish? It's all just gross and repulsive junk, right? Not exactly. In 2014, the EPA collected **data** about the kinds of refuse America produces. How do you think your own garbage measures up?

Most waste shown in the Garbage Pizza illustration below does not need to go to landfills. Paper, plastic, metal, and glass can be recycled. What about food scraps and yard trimmings? **Compost** them! They **decay** in compost heaps, turning into nutrient-rich soil.

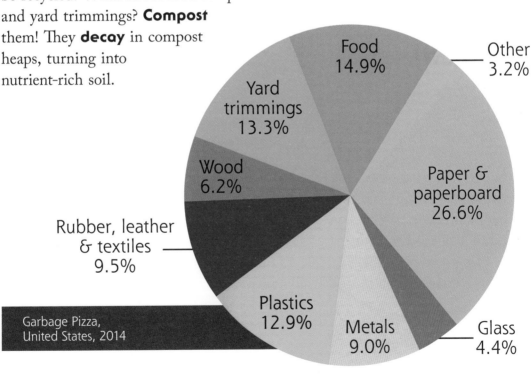

Food 14.9%
Other 3.2%
Yard trimmings 13.3%
Paper & paperboard 26.6%
Wood 6.2%
Rubber, leather & textiles 9.5%
Plastics 12.9%
Metals 9.0%
Glass 4.4%

Garbage Pizza, United States, 2014

WORDS TO KNOW

biodegradable: able to decay and break down.

decomposers: bacteria, fungi, and worms that break down wastes and dead plants and animals.

bacteria: microorganisms found in soil, water, plants, and animals. Some are harmful, while others are helpful.

fungi: mold, mildew, rust, and mushrooms. Plural of fungus.

nutrients: substances in food and soil that living things need to live and grow.

closed-loop life cycle: the life cycle for organic material that never comes to an end.

KINDS OF WASTE

What do you dump in your garbage? Does your trash contain more organic or inorganic waste?

Some mites act as decomposers.

Organic waste consists of plant and animal material, such as fallen leaves or potato peels. These materials are part of nature and were once alive. Organic waste is **biodegradable** and can be composted. It decays quickly with the help of **decomposers**.

DID YOU KNOW?

According to the United Nations, 1 billion people across the world will go to bed hungry tonight. Yet, each year in the United States, people throw out 96 billion pounds of food. Americans lead the world in food waste.

Decomposers are tiny, living recyclers such as **bacteria**, **fungi**, slugs, and worms. They feast on decaying plant and animal material, breaking them down into **nutrients** absorbed by the soil. These nutrients then become food for new plants and animals, and the circle of life continues. That's why organic waste has a **closed-loop life cycle**, which means it never actually ends.

Every hour of the day, Americans throw away 2.5 million plastic bottles. **Rock out to this video from GOOD and TakePart.com. Discover more about plastic's impact on our oceans.**

PS

🔍 GOOD use less plastic

Food scraps in a compost pile

credit: Philip Cohen (CC BY 2.0)

11

WORDS TO KNOW

festering: rotting.

putrid: decaying and smelling bad.

linear life cycle: the life cycle for inorganic material that comes to an end when it is thrown away.

toxin: a poisonous or harmful substance.

Food waste
credit: Petrr (CC BY 2.0)

Pewww! What makes that funky odor wafting from your trash? It's organic waste, such as **festering** fruits and veggies, **putrid** meats, and fish. As food scraps decay, they stink up garbage with a smell like rotten eggs.

Inorganic waste is not made from plants or animals. It doesn't break down quickly. Inorganic waste includes glass, plastics, and metals. Inorganic waste has a **linear life cycle**. When we throw it away, its life cycle ends.

Plastic waste such as this plastic bag drift throughout the oceans.
credit: Ben Mierement, NOAA NOS (ret.)

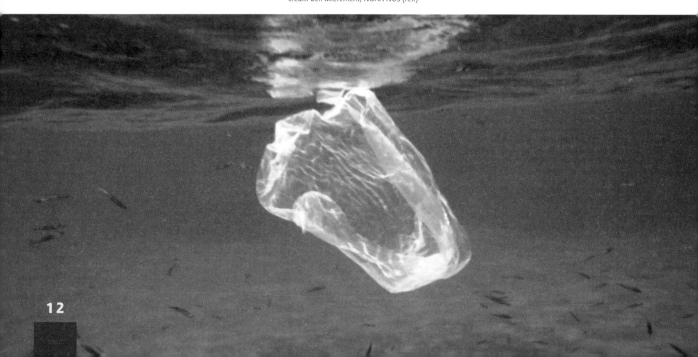

THE GREAT PACIFIC GARBAGE PATCH

There is a monstrosity that is three times the size of France and twice the size of Texas. It whirls in the Pacific Ocean between California and Hawaii. Experts estimate it contains more than 80,000 metric tons of rubbish. Glommed onto the enormous blob are shredded plastic bags, bobbing water bottles, and "ghost nets," which are abandoned fishing nets.

What in the world is it? It's a floating dump, a whirlpool of waste, a trash stew. It's the Great Pacific Garbage Patch. This is where lots of trash, produced by people around the world, collects together in a giant floating clump.

Mostly made of plastic, the drifting dump threatens animal life. In islands of junk, bags entangle dolphins. Turtles get trapped in abandoned fishing nets. Ducks and seabirds mistakenly gobble down plastic pellets. **Toxins** and chemicals in plastics poison animal life. Trash causes severe injuries and even death through choking or clogged intestines.

Discover more about the ways ocean plastic is "increasing exponentially" in this March 2018 article from the *Washington Post.* It includes a link to a video from National Ocean Services, "What Is the Great Pacific Garbage Patch?" Why is prevention the most important issue we must tackle?

PS

Washington Post Pacific garbage

WORDS TO KNOW

toxic: poisonous.

devour: to eat hungrily or greedily.

food chain: a community of animals and plants where each is eaten by another higher up in the chain.

marine: having to do with the ocean.

pollute: to make dirty or unclean with chemicals or other waste.

engineer: a person who uses science, math, and creativity to design and build things.

entrepreneur: a person who takes a risk to start and operate a business.

But that's not all. In the interconnected web of life of Earth, people are affected, too. Wind, waves, and sun break down the plastic into teeny pieces, like ingredients in a **toxic** stew.

This gross concoction not only chokes waters and threatens animal life— eventually, it also reaches us.

In diets worldwide, fish and shellfish are important sources of protein with excellent nutritional value. What happens when small fish, such as anchovies, ingest plastic? Chemicals build up in their body tissues. When larger fish, such as halibut and tuna, **devour** anchovies, chemicals keep on accumulating. Eventually, through the **food chain**, those larger fish reach our plates.

Living in a Plastic Ocean

Earth's precious oceans are filled with junk. **Marine** debris is man-made. People dump glass bottles and twisted cans, which bob over the water surface in garbage patches. They lose fishing gear that drifts to the ocean floor. An astonishing amount of marine debris is plastic, including smooshed water and shampoo bottles, sunscreen tubes, syringes, dilapidated toys, and diapers.

With friends and family, watch *Plastic Ocean*, produced by the United Nations. Share your observations and feelings about the video. Together, create an action plan to cut down on your use of plastics.

🔍 YouTube Plastic Ocean

RUBBISH ON LAND

You know how it can be really hard to fit even one more piece of trash into your garbage can at home? Sometimes that empty milk cartoon just won't squeeze in! That's when you know it's past time to take out the trash.

What does that mean on a global scale? Will there ever come a time when we just can't squeeze one more landfill into the planet? The question is pretty complex, and researchers haven't reached an agreement about the answer. One thing we have seen is what happens when individual states run out of room for their garbage—they put it on trucks and haul it away to other states that still have room.

For example, trash from New York City is shipped to landfills in Ohio, Pennsylvania, West Virginia, and elsewhere, where there is still plenty of room. While that might seem like a great solution, landfills in those states are going to eventually fill up, too. Plus, shipping garbage is another way we use energy that **pollutes** our planet.

DID YOU KNOW?

Americans toss enough trash to pack 63,000 garbage trucks—every day!

RUBBISH WARRIORS

Fresh ways of tackling challenges can change the world. Meet Boyan Slat, a 23-year-old inventor, **engineer**, and **entrepreneur** from Delft, in the Netherlands. His invention might end a global garbage problem.

Slat is the United Nations' youngest recipient of its greatest environmental honor, Champion of the Earth. During a diving trip to Greece when he was 16, Slat was astonished at what he encountered underwater. Plastic!

WORDS TO KNOW

technology: the tools, methods, and systems used to solve a problem or do work.

current: the steady flow of water or air in one direction.

propel: to drive or move forward.

feasibility: achievability.

"There were more plastic bags than fish," he said in an interview. "I realized it was a huge issue and that environmental issues are really the biggest problems my generation will face." Slat plunged himself into research. He learned that most conventional methods of cleaning ocean junk employed nets that filter the plastic from the water. Sadly, fish, turtles, and other marine life also became entangled in the nets.

Slat wondered, "What if there were an even better way?" He devoted himself to ridding the planet of ocean garbage patches. He founded The Ocean Cleanup, a group determined to develop new **technologies**.

The use of plastics has a devastating impact on our environment. **Explore the links at this website to read articles and view images from National Geographic.**

PS

🔎 National Geographic planet or plastic

credit: The Ocean Cleanup

He invented gigantic, solar-powered booms that rest on the ocean's surface and use the ocean's **currents**. As they slowly float, the booms act as barriers to drifting garbage.

The booms capture trash like huge funnels and propel it to their centers. Monthly, ships will collect the accumulated trash.

Slat presented a TED Talk and raised funds for his plan. After a six-year **feasibility** study, during which he tested, refined, and retested his invention, he launched the system in the Pacific Ocean in late 2018. "We need to intercept plastic before it becomes ocean plastic," Slat said. "And we need to clean up what is out there."

DID YOU KNOW?

In June 2018, an ailing pilot whale washed ashore on Thailand's southern coast. The gigantic mammal's belly was clogged with 18 pounds of plastic bags it had swallowed in the ocean. Though veterinarians battled to save the whale, it died. Yet, something positive came from this loss. It raised a red flag about our critical plastic problem. Why is awareness the first step in solving a problem?

Organic or Inorganic?

Look at this list of items many families might throw away. Decide if each is organic or inorganic waste.

- coffee grounds
- newspapers
- lettuce and tomato scraps
- hamburger buns
- batteries
- dryer lint
- plastic grocery bags
- scrap paper
- old magazines
- empty vitamin bottles
- empty tubes of toothpaste
- tubes from paper towels and toilet paper
- tea bags
- egg shells
- carrot and cucumber peels
- fabric softener sheets

ESSENTIAL QUESTION

Do you produce more inorganic or organic waste?

TRACK YOUR TRASH

What's in your rubbish? For one week, track and record every item your family discards. Be very careful because trash can contain broken or sharp objects.

❯ **Use a scale to weigh three large empty plastic tubs.** Record the weights in your science journal.

❯ **Reuse cardboard, index cards, or scratch paper to make three labels for the tubs:** "Trash," "Reusable," "Recyclable." Attach the labels to the tubs.

❯ **For one week, become your family's garbage collector.** Put on rubber gloves to rummage through every item of trash. **Be on the lookout for broken or sharp items and handle with care.** Categorize each as trash, reusable, or recyclable. Place each article in the appropriate container.

❯ **At the end of the week, weigh each tub of stuff.** Subtract the original weight of the empty tub from the total and record how much waste each tub has.

❯ **Compare and contrast your totals with those published by the EPA.** Did each person in your household produce about 31½ pounds of garbage, which is the national average?

❯ **Challenge your family to cut down your amount of garbage.** Rethink your trash choices. What can you reuse or recycle, instead of discarding? If you get a composter, you can compost food waste.

❯ **A month from now, try this activity again to observe your success.** Are your results different?

Try This!

Finished sorting and categorizing your garbage? Generate your own pie graph to illustrate your results. You can find graphs at this website.

🔎 NCES create graph

Chapter 2

HEAPS OF
HISTORY

THOUGHT YOU E GOING TO DO ESEARCH AT A ARBAGE DUMP?

I AM!

HEN WHY ARE YOU DRESSED LIKE AN ARCHAEOLOGIST?

I'M GOING ON A FIELD TRIP TO HUNT FOR ARTIFACTS AT AN ANCIENT TRASH HEAP.

ARCHAEOLOGISTS LOVE ANCIENT GARBAGE. IT TELLS THEM A LOT ABOUT HOW PEOPLE USED TO LIVE.

SO WHAT'S THE DIFFERENCE BETWEEN GARBAGE AND AN ARTIFACT?

I'D GUESS ABOUT A THOUSAND YEARS!

Throughout human history, people have dumped lots of rubbish. To archaeologists, ancient discarded garbage isn't junk. It's treasure! Random odds and ends people threw away long ago are now considered artifacts.

Artifacts reveal amazing insights about how people used to live and are just as valuable to researchers as dazzling jewels. That's why **middens**, what we call ancient garbage dumps, are prime places for archaeologists to dig. These trash pits are packed with bones and shells from ancient meals, along with fragments of stone tools, pottery, and wood.

SSENTIAL QUESTION

ow has garbage umping changed hroughout history?

Excavators digging at a kitchen midden at Elizabeth Island in the Strait of Magellan

PREHISTORIC PEOPLE ON THE MOVE

Our ancestors were hunter-gatherers. Millions of years ago, these **nomadic** people moved from place to place with the seasons. Several families banded together in small groups and journeyed from one area to another to find food and freshwater sources.

Imagine you're a hunter-gatherer. What does your family do with garbage? Piles it in a cave to decay! With frequent moves, you don't have enough time to produce heaps of waste in one place. Sure, there's ash from fires. Leftovers from meals. But this trash is organic. It decays over time, returning nutrients to soil. It's a closed-loop life cycle, healthy for the planet.

DID YOU KNOW?

Trash contains treasures! Archaeologists **excavated** a site in ancient Arsuf, north of Tel Aviv in Israel. They unearthed coins, jewelry and **intact** lamps from a Byzantine trash heap.

The trash produced by people millions of years ago was different from the trash we produce now.

Plastic hadn't been invented yet! Neither had rubber, or glass, or asphalt. People wore biodegradable animal skins on their bodies and feet. They made bags out of animal skin, too. All the waste they created broke down and reduced to nothing.

During the next 5,000 years, however, larger groups of people settled down in one place and started farming. That's when trash troubles began to kick in. Folks needed to figure out where to leave all their garbage.

Ancient Clambakes

Shell middens are remains of ancient dinners that hunter-gatherers left behind! Shell middens are located around the world's coastlines, where **edible** mollusks thrive. For example, they are found along rivers, streams, and lagoons. These food sources were relatively easy for hunter-gatherers to scoop up.

When archaeologists excavate and investigate giant heaps of clam, mussel, and oyster shells, they discover ways in which food was prepared. Ancient people steamed and baked their shellfish—as we do today.

Shell midden in Argentina

DID YOU KNOW?

Do tell! Ancient cities in the Middle East rose on top of human-made hills called **tells**. Heaps of garbage and artifacts, including coins and ceramics, are buried inside tells.

ANCIENT CIVILIZATIONS SETTLED DOWN

Eventually, large groups of people settled in thriving cities. Naturally, bigger groups produced more garbage. Tons more.

There was no garbage collection back then. So, people simply dumped trash right on the floors of their homes. How do we know? Archaeologists have excavated houses in the ancient city of Troy, located in present-day Turkey. People lived in Troy 3,000 to 4,000 years ago. Archaeologists unearthed layers of animal bones left from meals munched long ago.

If you lived during that time, you'd finish eating and plop your gnawed bones onto the clay floor. What happened when a floor became slimy and rancid? Your family slathered it with a fresh layer of earth and clay. You piled on more garbage, squashed it underfoot until it got too revolting, and repeated the process, again and again.

Ruins of Troy
credit: David Spender (CC BY 2.0)

Sometimes, all the rubbish didn't fit on cramped floors. Then, it was time to throw it out of the house. People chucked larger chunks of stuff straight out doors or windows and right onto streets. Wandering pigs, famished cats, and packs of dogs waded through slippery gunk to devour rotting leftovers.

When too much trash blocked streets, it was time to burn it, bury it, or haul it off to putrid dumps on village outskirts. People also threw garbage into lakes, rivers, and oceans. Good riddance to bad rubbish. Or so they thought.

People didn't realize the impact their behavior had on one another and on the environment. Their actions caused horrible smells and polluted water supplies. They created ideal conditions for deadly diseases to spread.

WASTING AWAY FROM DISEASE

Not only did the careless way of dealing with waste cause people to hold their noses a lot, it also caused many, many deaths.

During the **Middle Ages**, 1,000 years ago, city populations boomed in Europe. So did garbage and filthy conditions. Unfortunately, people didn't realize there was a link between filth and public health.

Raise the Roof!

In the ancient city of Troy, people piled so many layers of garbage on their floors, they eventually had to make their roofs higher. And it didn't stop there. As mountains of rubbish rose higher and higher, so did the entire city. New buildings sprang up on top of trash heaps. Plus, whenever the city was flattened, either by natural disaster or invading armies, survivors rebuilt the area on top of the resulting heaps of waste. When modern archaeologists began to conduct digs on the site of the ancient city, they numbered the layers Troy I, Troy II, and so on, all the way up to Troy IX.

WORDS TO KNOW

chamber pot: a jug or bowl stashed under beds as a personal port-a-potty.

slaughterhouse: a place where animals are killed for food.

vermin: small animals or insects that are pests, such as cockroaches or mice.

bubonic plague: a deadly infectious disease carried by rats and mice that can spread to humans. Also called Black Death.

biological warfare: using toxins and infectious agents as weapons of war.

catapult: weapon of war used to launch objects over a great distance.

corpse: a dead body.

feces: poop.

epidemic: a disease that hits large groups at the same time and spreads quickly.

infectious: able to spread quickly from one person to others.

Chamber pot from the nineteenth century

Streets were like open toilets, where people flung human waste from **chamber pots**. In disgustingly dirty cities, human and animal waste mixed with horse droppings and bloody guts that **slaughterhouses** workers dumped in streets. People burned trash, heaped it into giant mounds, or plopped it into water. Or they just walked around festering garbage and struggled to ignore the horrific stench.

In this toxic environment, rats and other **vermin** thrived. Fleas carried a deadly disease called **bubonic plague**. In the mid-1400s, rats carried infected fleas throughout Europe's cities and villages. Fleas hopped off rats and onto people, biting them and infecting them with the plague.

DID YOU KNOW?

More than 2,000 years ago, the people of Pompeii in Italy tossed reeking rubbish and human waste into streets. Workers paved streets and walkways with rugged steppingstones. As people strode from stone to stone, they stayed high and dry. Their robes and sandals didn't slosh through the goo.

Biological Warfare

Throughout history, people used the plague as a ghastly weapon of **biological warfare**. During the Middle Ages, people employed **catapults** to hurl both plague-ridden **corpses** and their infected **feces** over castle walls and beyond fortified city walls. Contagion swept through cities. It advanced the terrible disease and left more corpses in its wake. What happened to people who managed to flee in desperation? They spread the plague to other areas. The Black Death marched on.

In this way, the plague galloped through the streets like a racehorse. Called the Black Death because it caused black spots on the skin, the plague was one of the most devastating **epidemics** in history. The Black Death wiped out nearly 60 percent of Europe's population between 1348 and 1350. It killed a total of 75 million people worldwide.

Microscopes hadn't been invented yet, so doctors had no idea what caused the **infectious** disease. Some insisted it was the evil eye. Others thought it was caused by mysterious vapors, or bad air, wafting from the planets. Fearing for their own lives, doctors stopped treating the sick. Abandoned by sick owners, dogs, chickens, sheep, and oxen died, too.

In time, the grisly plague ran its course. A major positive consequence grew from the Black Death: People began making a connection between filthy garbage and the spread of disease.

A plague doctor

WORDS TO KNOW

sewer: a drain for wastewater.

wastewater: dirty water that has been used by people in their homes, in factories, and in other businesses.

yellow fever: a disease caused by a virus spread through mosquito bites.

delirious: a condition of restlessness, confusion, and excitement brought on by a high fever, often with mixed-up speech.

slops: a mushy mixture of kitchen scraps and liquid fed to pigs.

sanitation: conditions relating to public health and cleanliness.

possessions: things you own.

manufactured: made by machines.

thrift: using money carefully.

deforestation: the process through which forests are cleared to use land for other purposes.

climate change: a change in long-term weather patterns, which can happen through natural or man-made processes.

ecosystem: an interdependent community of living and nonliving things and their environment.

Europe in the Middle Ages wasn't the only place where garbage caused serious disease. In 1793, it happened in the United States in Philadelphia, Pennsylvania.

At that time, the bustling port city of Philadelphia was the nation's capital. Ditches called "sinks," or open **sewers**, flowed through unpaved streets carrying **wastewater**. On this trail of guck, a deadly **yellow fever** epidemic spread through the city during a broiling hot summer.

Yellow fever came from Africa and traveled to other parts of the world through the slave trade. Symptoms were horrible. Victims' bones rattled with violent shakes. After a few days, their eyeballs and skin turned yellow. Their noses and gums bled. They vomited black blood. **Delirious** with a raging fever, they babbled nonsense for hours. After a few miserable days, they died.

As with the Black Death, doctors didn't know what caused yellow fever. They didn't realize infectious mosquitoes that thrived in the city's swamps and sinks were the source. After a three-month rampage, the epidemic stopped when cold weather killed the mosquitoes. People finally made a connection between filth and disease and improved **sanitation**. In 1799, America's first clean-water system was started in Philadelphia.

DID YOU KNOW?

Pig out! In early America, pigs enjoyed jobs as living garbage disposals. Settlers fed them **slops**, a mushy mixture of leftover food and kitchen debris. Some towns depended on pigs to get rid of practically all their garbage! Did you know a drove, or group, of pigs can devour a ton of trash a day?

WASTE NOT, WANT NOT

When settlers arrived in America in the early 1600s, they had few **possessions**. **Manufactured** goods were expensive. People valued **thrift**. They pinched pennies, spent money carefully, and didn't waste what they bought. What they did have was precious to them. What happened to chipped cups and saucers? They weren't thrown away. Instead, folks painstakingly patched them with egg whites, glue, or clay.

Settlers also used food creatively. After cooking beef and chicken, people stashed leftover animal fat in grease jars. When they had enough, they used it to make soap. Beets and onions bubbling in supper pots produced delicious soup as well as bright dyes for clothing. And after brewing a kettle of evening tea, settlers scooped out the tea leaves to reuse in the next day's pot. When the taste was all boiled away, they dried the leaves and scattered them on the floors to soak up dust.

Climate Change Corner

Trees of Life

Now, scientists know **deforestation** is a major contributor to **climate change**. But the first settlers in North America deliberately altered **ecosystems** to *create* climate change! When settlers journeyed to the New World, they expected a mild climate like the one they were accustomed to in Europe. They envisioned clear water and lush landscapes filled with abundant fruit. Instead, they found miles of thick, rugged wilderness and mucky swamplands. Winters were bitterly cold and snowy. Hot summers were soggy with humidity.

In a misguided plan, settlers attempted to tame the climate through deforestation—fast. Settlers burned or chopped down millions of trees and cleared away thick underbrush. Communities joined together to roll massive logs into piles and burn them in fires that smoldered for days. Then, settlers drained marshes and built dams. They introduced European farming methods to the cleared land. But the plan backfired. In reality, people destroyed precious resources. Their cleared lands grew colder in the winters and hotter in the summers.

WORDS TO KNOW

resourceful: able to think of creative solutions to problems.

salvaged: recovered parts or materials that are recycled or reused.

industrialized: when there is a lot of manufacturing. Products are made by machines in large factories.

ration: to limit the amount of something to be used each week or month.

victory garden: a garden planted by Americans during World War II. About 2 million victory gardens produced 40 percent of the food grown in the United States during the war.

Industrial Revolution: the name of the period of time that started in England in the late 1700s when people started using machines to make things in large factories.

non-renewable: a natural resource that can be used up, that we can't make more of, such as oil.

greenhouse gas: a gas that traps heat in the earth's atmosphere and contributes to the greenhouse effect and global warming.

carbon dioxide: a gas formed by the burning of fossil fuels, the rotting of plants and animals, and the breathing out of animals or humans.

fossil fuel: a natural fuel that formed long ago from the remains of living organisms. Oil, natural gas, and coal are fossil fuels.

Only the wealthy could afford changes of clothing. Fabric was expensive, so people had to be **resourceful**. Most people had only one or two sets of clothes. Sewing was an important skill that girls learned at a young age. Women mended dresses repeatedly with **salvaged** pieces of mismatched fabrics.

Some clothing was such a mix of scraps that people resembled walking quilts.

Because people used their resources so sparingly, there wasn't much waste. How do these descriptions compare with the way you buy, wear, use, and get rid of clothing, household items, and food you don't eat?

INDUSTRIALIZATION AND BEYOND

After the Civil War ended in 1865, the United States became increasingly **industrialized**. Prices of manufactured products started to drop. As items became cheaper and easier to acquire, people bought more of them. And they left farming to work in cities, where they could earn more money in factories.

Now that people were working away from home, they looked for ways to save time. They bought bread rather than baking it. They could afford new shirts instead of patching old ones. Families purchased many more packaged goods. These new products created more and more garbage.

During World War II, Americans on the home front pitched in to help save resources that could help the war effort. They **rationed** food and gas and planted **victory gardens** to grow fruits and vegetables. From coast to coast, people chanted, "Use it up, wear it out, make it do, or do without." Have you or your family ever had to be very careful with your resources? How did it make you think differently about what you threw out?

The Industrial Revolution and Climate Change

Prior to the **Industrial Revolution** (1760–1840), people produced mostly organic waste. They labored to make their own necessities and hung on to precious possessions. In addition, pre-industrial societies used energy created through wind, water, and burning wood. After the Industrial Revolution, however, as a throw-away consumer culture emerged, climate change was impacted, too. The world's population exploded. People cleared forests, built housing, and expanded cities. For the first time, people turned to a **non-renewable** energy source: coal. Since then, an excess of **greenhouse gases** such as **carbon dioxide** has meant continually rising temperatures. Watch *Climate Change 101 With Bill Nye* to learn about **fossil fuels** burned during the Industrial Revolution and our use of those fuels today.

🔎 Climate Change 101 Bill Nye

WORDS TO KNOW

consumerism: a willingness to spend money on goods and services.

suburb: where people live near a city.

hype: excitement through a hard-sell approach.

After World War II ended in 1945, Americans experienced even more new wealth and **consumerism**. Many moved out of cities to large, growing **suburbs**. Ads and commercials urged people to buy more new and improved products. Disposable items promised people cheap convenience. Americans bought into the **hype**.

Re-Maya

The ancient Maya reused and recycled. They salvaged hunks of broken pottery from homes and stones from buildings to construct temples. The Maya also reduced their use of resources in burial practices. Instead of burying the dead with solid gold earrings, bracelets, and necklaces, they wrapped gold foil around clay beads to make fabulous fakes.

 Learn more about the Maya in this video. What can we learn from this culture?

🔍 Nat Geo Maya

It continues today, as online shopping makes it quick and easy to snag new purchases. Many people buy large amounts of material goods. What topped purchase lists in 2017? Disposables such as paper towels and cinnamon toothpaste, small appliances including pressure cookers and juicers. Wireless headphones were biggies, and so were waterproof phone cases. Even robotic vacuum cleaners. More and more and more stuff!

Where will we dump everything when we're finished with it? How will all this garbage affect our environment—and our future?

How many devices does your family replace every year?

credit: takomabibelot (CC BY 2.0)

ESSENTIAL QUESTION

How has garbage dumping changed throughout history?

TO DYE FOR!

Has your old T-shirt seen better days? No need to let it die. Dye it instead! Next time your family boils colorful veggies, don't dump the water. Use it to brew natural dyes the way colonists and pioneers did. Then, use those dyes to jazz up your shirt and give it new life.

Caution: This activity requires boiling water, so have an adult help you.

❯ **Choose your color.** Beets will make red. Carrots produce orange. Gold onions make yellow, red cabbage produces purple, and spinach gives you green. Put the vegetables in a pot, cover with water, and boil them. Drain the liquid and strain out any solid bits. Store the liquid in a glass jar until you're ready to dye the shirt.

❯ **Before you use your colored liquid, you'll need to make sure the dye will set in the fabric.** Pour 4 cups of cold water and 1 cup of vinegar into a large pot. Place the T-shirt into the mixture. Then, put the pot on the stove and simmer the shirt for a full hour. Check on it now and then to make sure the mixture doesn't boil away. After an hour, remove the shirt and rinse it in cold water.

❯ **Now you're ready to work with your dye.** Return the pot and T-shirt to the stove and pour in the colored water. Simmer again. When you are happy with the color of the shirt, turn off the heat. Wear rubber gloves to handle the shirt because dye stains skin. The color will dry a few shades lighter than it looks in the pot. **Hint:** When it's time to launder your shirt, wash it separately in cold water. The dye will last longer and won't stain anything else.

DID YOU KNOW?

In the Middle Ages, dyers soaked fabrics in vats of old urine to set dyes!

Try This!

Read *From Gunpowder to Teeth Whitener: The Science Behind Historic Uses of Urine*. How did preindustrial humans use urine to develop industries? With a friend or family member, discuss the science behind the power of pee.

🔎 From Gunpowder to Teeth Whitener

STENCH B-GONE POMANDER

In colonial times, people used **pomanders** to ward off bad odors. Some people believed pomanders protected them from disease. Make a pomander with citrus fruit and cloves. It's a fantastic, spicy air-freshener made with all-natural products.

❯ **Use a nail or skewer to carefully pierce a pattern into a medium-sized orange or large lemon.** Try squiggles, zigzags, diamonds, or hearts. If you prefer, just pierce holes all over the fruit.

❯ **Fill each hole with a clove.** You'll need about a half cup of whole cloves. Each time you press a spicy clove into the fruit, you'll catch a whiff of mingled scents. Watch your fingers and pushing thumb. Cloves can be sharp and prickly.

❯ **After you finish adding cloves, set the fruit aside.** Pour a tablespoon each of cinnamon, nutmeg, allspice, and ginger in a paper bag. Add a tablespoon of orris root powder, which preserves the pomander's scent. Shake the bag to mingle all the ingredients.

❯ **Place the fruit in the bag and roll it in the spices.** Remove the fruit and tie a ribbon around it. Hang the pomander and allow it to dry out for about a week. Then, hang it in the kitchen or a closet to freshen the air.

Try This!

Read about the ways pomanders were used in the past, and check out a 1495 illustration of a doctor using a pomander to ward off the plague.

🔎 Pomanders and the Plague

WORDS TO KNOW

pomander: ball or perforated container that holds scented materials.

DIG IT!

Archaeologists dig through layers of soil to scout for artifacts. Bury some artifacts in a shoebox, create layers, and peel away the box to reveal your own dig site.

❯ **Gather small artifacts from your life, such as coins, keys, game pieces, jewelry, broken toys, washed chicken bones.** Use them to make an artifact layer. Spread odds and ends along the bottom of a shoebox. Add about ½ cup of cornstarch into a spray bottle of water. Shake well. Spray the artifact layer with the water mixture.

❯ **Collect some dirt from outdoors.** In a large bowl or tub, combine most of the dirt with birdseeds or sesame seeds and spread it over the artifacts. Leave some extra dirt aside. Spray this soil layer with the water-cornstarch mixture until it has the consistency of a soggy mudpie. It should move and flow a bit.

❯ **Collect sand, gravel, and pebbles.** Combine most of it with water until it is moist. Leave some extra sand aside. Spread the mixture over the soil layer. Press down firmly so materials stick together. **Hint:** If layers aren't sticking together well enough, add a bit more cornstarch to the water to thicken it.

❯ **Combine the remaining dirt and sand.** Spray with the water mixture and press onto the sand layer. Then, sprinkle plant findings, such as twigs, bark, leaves, grass, pinecones, pine needles, acorns, and flowers, over the top. Set the shoebox aside and wait three full days for your model to dry thoroughly. If you live somewhere humid, it could take longer.

❯ **After the model has dried, use scissors to cut down the shoebox's corners.** Leave the bottom intact. Carefully pull away all four sides to unveil your model.

Consider This!

Skilled archaeologists use precise processes to dig through layers of soil to excavate sites and unearth artifacts. How might amateur "treasure hunters" actually destroy valuable sites as they dig on their own?

INVESTIGATE A MINI MIDDEN

Pretend you're an archaeologist from the future. Dig into a wastebasket from the present and carefully examine the artifacts you find. What do they tell you about how people live today?

❯ **Before you begin, come up with a list of questions to guide you in your investigation.** Jot them in your science journal. You might include questions such as these.

✱ Who used these items?

✱ What foods did they eat?

✱ What animals did they live with?

✱ How did they dress?

❯ **In the notebook, make a chart with three column headings:** "Sketch," "Description," "Use."

❯ **Spread out a plastic sheet or tarp and carefully unload the wastebasket onto it.** Use a pair of rubber gloves, and beware of anything sharp or broken as you carefully separate items.

❯ **For each item, complete the chart.** Write a description and make a quick sketch. Then, think about how the item might have been used and who used it.

❯ **Once you finish your excavation, look again at the list of questions** you wrote down and draw conclusions about the folks who produced this rubbish.

DID YOU KNOW?

Some archaeologists are **garbologists**. They dig through landfills to study the garbage a society produced, especially household waste.

Try This!

Ask permission from a family member to investigate their wastebasket. That way, you'll explore unfamiliar stuff discarded by others.

WORDS TO KNOW

garbologist: an archaeologist who studies garbage.

Chapter 3

WHERE DOES
TRASH GO?

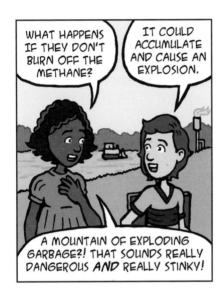

Take out the trash. Throw away the garbage. Dump the junk. Sooner or later, no matter where you live, you must get rid of your rubbish.

Look around your home or classroom right now. Everything you see will eventually need to be tossed out. What are you going to do with your granola bar wrapper? What about those pencil stubs? How about that chewed piece of gum? Where are all of these things going to end up?

SSENTIAL QUESTION

/hat role do landfills
lay in solid-waste
nanagement?

Once you make the decision to ditch something, it enters the **waste stream**. This is the flow of garbage to its final destination. Garbage can be recycled or burned. But many people choose to dump it. So where does dumped junk go?

35

WORDS TO KNOW

waste stream: the flow of household and industrial garbage that gets hauled away, recycled, incinerated, or disposed of in landfills.

sanitation worker: a person hired to collect and dispose of garbage.

compactor: a machine that tightly packs trash.

compress: to squeeze and squish things to make them smaller.

cell: a storage space for garbage in a landfill.

There's no magical spot where garbage vanishes in a poof. "Away" is somewhere. That somewhere is usually a landfill in your town or neighborhood.

OUT AND AWAY TO THE LANDFILL

If it weren't for landfills, you'd be slogging through slime. Friends and family would plod over squishy, awful mounds of goo. Landfills save us from this fate!

A landfill in Australia

36

According to the EPA, the United States boasts 3,091 active landfills in current use and another 10,000 closed municipal landfills. You've probably spotted landfills along highways near your community. **Check out the "How Much Trash Is Near Your Home?" interactive map from this website.** Enter the addresses of your home, school, and other places in your community. Where are "Craters of Waste" located? Were you aware of them? How do they impact your area?

🔍 land of waste

As part of solid-waste management, garbage trucks pick up trash and haul it away to landfills. Imagine you're a **sanitation worker** in a rumbling truck named Bertha. Bertha bellows a warning and chugs down long streets to visit every house and apartment building. You stop at each, picking up hefty cans and plastic bags and hurling them into a **compactor** at the truck's rear. Like monster jaws, the compactor chomps and **compresses** trash.

Bertha holds a gigantic 14 tons of waste. This is about as much trash as 850 households produce! When the truck fills to the brim with compacted junk, you hit the landfill. Shrieking seagulls circle overhead. You blast your horn to shoo them away. Seagulls rummage through debris and scatter litter to the wind. Surrounded by the stench of rotting food, you dump your truckload into a **cell**. This is a storage space for garbage. Soon, it's time to rumble off to another neighborhood and another stretch of waiting cans and bags of trash.

DID YOU KNOW?

New York's Fresh Kills landfill once towered at a height of 225 feet tall. That's taller than the Statue of Liberty! After Fresh Kills closed in 2001, New York City needed to ship its trash away. Now, the city's garbage travels to landfills and incinerators in New Jersey, Virginia, Ohio, and South Carolina.

PARTS OF A LANDFILL

A landfill is more than just a dump. It's a garbage graveyard. On the surface, it looks like a gargantuan trash hill. As you've already learned, an open dump allows disease to spread, while a landfill helps protect the environment.

Engineers and scientists use current technology to design landfills that protect people and the planet.

It takes massive earthmovers to build a landfill. First, backhoes dig an enormous trench, or underground cell, about 200 feet wide and up to a half-mile deep. This massive hole in the ground is the storage compartment for trash. Backhoes shove aside removed soil to reuse later.

You can't just dump garbage into this hole, though. Trash often contains toxic materials such as battery acids and **pesticides**. Other items, such as disposable tableware, leak **contaminants** as they break down. As waste decomposes, it produces **leachate**. This liquid mixes with rainwater to brew a toxic soup.

To keep the toxic soup from seeping into the ground, the bottom of the landfill contains a layer of clay. This protects soil and **groundwater** from **contamination**. On top of the clay layer is a heavy plastic liner for extra protection.

DID YOU KNOW?

Landfills emit the greenhouse gas **methane**. Methane can provide energy. Some communities capture methane coming from landfills and use it to generate heat and electricity.

Mountains of Trash

India is the second-most populous country in the world, with a population of 1.35 billion. You know that wherever there are people, there is garbage. An enormous population produces an enormous amount of waste. In fact, some of India's largest cities are the largest producers of garbage in the world. People generate a whopping 62 million tons of trash, dumping it on streets and other public spaces. Only about 82 percent of that trash is collected. Of that, only 28 percent gets processed. There is little recycling. And literal mountains of trash.

Cities battle huge sanitation problems. In the last two decades, for example, Delhi experienced an explosion in the amount of garbage produced. People dump trash in open dumps, where they burn rubbish. Air and groundwater become polluted. That presents a public health hazard.

Goa, a state in western India, has a population of nearly 1.5 million. In Goa's village of Aldona, schoolkids pitch in to solve the garbage problem now and for the future. Watch the video to see them in action! How do they use recycling to make a difference?

🔍 YouTube Garbage in Goa

Installed above the liner is a layer of pipes. Pipes collect **runoff** rainwater and leachate. The pipes also serve another purpose. When garbage rots in the landfill, it releases a gas called methane. Methane is **flammable**. It can be explosive if too much builds up in a contained space. To reduce the danger of an explosion, pipes carry methane outside, where it is released into the air.

It takes a sanitation worker only five minutes to unload a mammoth garbage trailer! In some places, garbage trucks transfer trash to barges, which are large boats with flat bottoms. Then, tugboats push barges across water to landfills.

After garbage trucks tip their loads into refuse cells, the landfill compactor attacks. At 84,000 pounds and armed with spiky metal wheels, this bad boy means business. The compactor rolls over garbage again and again, squashing it to make room for more loads.

When the compactor finishes its work, the bulldozer roars into action. Remember the soil that the backhoes set aside? Now the bulldozer pushes this dirt and spreads it over all the garbage. This top soil layer, called daily cover, keeps hungry scavengers such as rats, raccoons, and coyotes from scrounging for supper. It also puts a lid on foul odors.

In the morning, workers rev up their engines and start the process all over again.

Landfill compactor

Climate Change Corner

Methane Gone Mad

The more trash we dump in landfills, the more we impact climate change. You read that methane is a greenhouse gas. It's often generated by human activities. As organic materials decay in landfills, they cause methane **emissions**. In fact, the EPA estimates landfills are the third-greatest cause of methane emissions in the United States, behind fossil-fuel production and use and **livestock** farming.

It takes about 30 to 50 years for a landfill to reach **capacity**. When it's maxed out, waste disposal companies close it. Even when buried, decaying garbage can harm air and water, so companies keep a watchful eye on closed landfills. In fact, local, state, and federal laws require a minimum **monitoring** period of 30 years.

Once closed, a landfill becomes part of your community. **Repurposed**, it can morph into a grassy recreational area, such as a golf course, baseball diamond, or park. Some closed landfills become nature preserves or areas with trails for running, walking, and horseback riding.

Mount Trashmore Park, Virginia Beach, a repurposed landfill
credit: Bdmccray (CC BY 2.0)

We're still layering our trash like people did back in Troy—and we're running out of room.

In 1990, there were 6,300 landfills in the United States. Now, as you read this, there are only about 3,091. Another will close today because it's full. It's important to reduce, reuse, and recycle, so we jam way less stuff into garbage graveyards.

WORDS TO KNOW

dioxin: an extremely toxic chemical that can be released from burning some materials.

dubious: doubtful, uncertain.

jettison: to throw something away.

algae: a simple organism found in water that is like a plant but without roots, stems, or leaves.

Landfills are the most common solution to waste management problems in terms of everyday household trash that comes from homes, businesses, and construction sites. But what about the kind of waste that can cause serious health concerns? What about chemicals and toxins that can hurt people and animals? What do we do with these waste products? We'll find out more in the next chapter.

DID YOU KNOW?

When garbage gets incinerated, it doesn't just go up in smoke. Garbage can release chemicals such as **dioxin** if it's not burned properly. That's the most toxic human-made substance on the planet. In addition, ash is left behind that needs to be disposed of—in a landfill.

RUBBISH WARRIORS

The United States boasts a **dubious** distinction. It leads the world in a mind-boggling amount of food waste. We dump about 60 million tons of produce a year. That's $160 billion worth of fruits and vegetables **jettisoned** to landfills! In fact, wasted food takes up the greatest amount of space in landfills.

Back when Mackenzie Cowles was in fifth grade at Greenbrook Elementary School in Danville, California, she decided to do something about all that food waste. Her class tracked and weighed garbage dumped in the cafeteria. Mackenzie and her classmates couldn't believe what kids threw out—full juice boxes, unopened bags of chips, whole bananas, oranges, and apples. Even ice packs!

Visit Tomoko Landfill near Daytona Beach, Florida. **Watch Life at the Landfill for the sights and sounds of a landfill in action.**

(PS)

YouTube life at landfill

Mackenzie's class challenged the entire school to reduce waste and help the environment. They designed posters and held a no-waste lunch. Her class created a share basket. If someone didn't eat a banana, for example, they placed it in the share basket. If kids forgot to bring lunch or felt extra hungry, they could grab something out of the basket.

Years later, Mackenzie recalls how the project changed her actions. "Now, when I eat or drink, I take only the amount I can finish," she explained. "If there's something left in my lunch, I don't throw it away. I save it in my backpack and eat it for a snack later. It's really important to help the planet. Good things come back."

ESSENTIAL QUESTION

What role do landfills play in solid-waste management?

Dead Zone

Nothing survives in a dead zone. Dead zones are areas in oceans where oxygen levels are so low life can't be sustained. Every summer, a dead zone the size of New Jersey forms in the Gulf of Mexico. Cow manure and chemical fertilizers from farms in the Midwest wash into the Mississippi River. They create the marine wasteland when they seep into groundwater and flow to the Gulf. There, chemicals cause massive **algae** growth beyond what is normal. As blankets of algae decompose, they suck oxygen from water. Fish and shrimp must move to cleaner waters to breathe. Sadly, they don't all make it. Thousands of fish perish in the Gulf. The dead zone becomes a carpet of dead fish. In 2017, the National Oceanic and Atmospheric Association (NOAA) reported that the dead zone sprawled to 8,776 square miles. That's the largest expanse reported since mapping in 1985.

Read this feature from NOAA to discover more. Why is measuring the dead zone critical?

🔎 Gulf of Mexico dead zone

SIMULATE WATER POLLUTION

Landfills are designed to seal in waste that might contaminate water. Yet toxic dust can still escape and blow into water sources. These pollutants spread quickly, sinking into soil and washing up on beaches. In this experiment, use a stalk of celery to find out how plants take in and circulate water pollution. Have an adult help you cut the celery.

❯ **Fill a clear glass jar halfway with water.** Add eight drops of food coloring. Red or blue works better than other colors for this activity. Imagine that the color is a pesticide that flowed from a backyard into a pond.

❯ **Carefully pour dirt into the jar and stir the mixture.** Think of the dirt as cigarette ashes that picnickers ditched in the pond.

❯ **Choose a stalk of celery that's light in color and has leaves.** Wash the stalk to remove any traces of dirt. Then cut off a bit of the bottom. Pretend the celery is a healthy tree growing at the water's edge. Place the stalk into the jar with the leaves pointing up. Allow the celery to remain in the water overnight. Start a scientific method worksheet and predict what will happen.

❯ **The next day, take the celery out of the jar.** What happened to the leaves? To the stalk?

DID YOU KNOW?

The Sarno River in Italy is Europe's most polluted river. People have dumped garbage into it, along with untreated industrial wastes. Conditions impact nearly 1 million residents! Italy started dredging to clean up the river and installed floating booms to capture oil and garbage.

Try This!

Cut away several samples of the celery to study. Do you see colored lines or dots of dirt in the stalk's veins? What conclusions can you draw about water pollution?

SNAG AIR POLLUTION ON A STICK-IT CAN

What's hovering in the air where you live? Find out! Go outside and grab air pollution with a sticky can. What can you snatch in a week? Start a scientific method worksheet to organize your experiment.

❯ **Select two equal-sized cans to reuse.** Wash them and soak or peel off labels before thoroughly drying the cans.

❯ **Choose two different outdoor areas to test.** How about the top of a tree stump in your yard or the ledge of a window near your apartment? Write the locations on the cans.

❯ **Fill the cans with gravel and stones to provide weight so they don't blow away outside.** Then use double-sided tape to cover the outside of the cans. Try to keep your fingerprints, fuzzballs, and pet hairs off the tape. It's tricky!

❯ **Now you're ready to capture air pollution on your stick-it cans.** At each outdoor location, use your senses to observe air conditions. What do you smell? How does the air look and feel? Are there factories or chimneys nearby? Burning leaves? Is someone grilling burgers?

❯ **Wait a full week.** Check every day to make sure the cans haven't been disturbed. After a week, use a magnifying glass to study the samples. Record your observations in your science journal. What's stuck on the tape? Do you observe particles of ash, dust, or soot? How about bits of plants, pollen, or other items that aren't examples of pollution? Any liquids? Anything you can't identify? What could it be?

❯ **Compare and contrast the cans.** Which sample grabbed more pollution? What outdoor conditions affected the results? Draw conclusions about your findings.

Try This!

Ask a friend to test two different locations. Compare and contrast your findings.

BREAK IT DOWN WITH BIODEGRADATION

Biodegradable materials decay and decompose with help from bacteria and sunlight. Collect kitchen scraps for this two-week activity. Start a scientific method worksheet in your science journal and predict which items will break down most quickly when you bury them in test containers. Make sure you have permission from an adult to dig a hole in the ground! Use gloves to handle the garbage.

❯ **Gather organic and inorganic test materials.** Organic materials might include food scraps such as apple cores, banana peels, cantaloupe and watermelon rinds, carrot and potato peels, coffee grounds, and egg shells. Inorganic waste might include aluminum foil, juice bags, metal bottle caps, plastic grocery bags, plastic wrap, small glass jars, and Styrofoam. Divide the organic and inorganic materials into two fairly equal piles, mixing organic and inorganic items. **Hint:** Don't bury meat, fish, or bones, because hungry critters will dig up your experiment!

❯ **Make two charts in your science notebook, one for each pile.** The charts should have five columns. In the first, list the items you placed into each pile. Then, add three column headings: "no change," "some biodegradation," "major biodegradation."

item	no change	some biodegradation	major biodegradation	How accurate was my prediction?

❯ **Predict what will happen to each item and make a check mark in the appropriate column.** Add a last column: "How accurate was my prediction?"

❯ **Fill paper bags with samples.** Make sure materials are loosely packed rather than tightly squished together. Number the tags 1 and 2 and attach each to the appropriate bag. Snap pictures of both bags so you have a point of comparison when you dig the bags back up!

❯ **Choose a spot outdoors to bury the bags.** Dig two individual holes. Place each bag in a hole and cover it completely with soil. Water each thoroughly. Every day for two weeks, sprinkle the ground where the bags are buried with 2 quarts of water.

❯ **After two weeks, dig up the bags.** Spread a tarp outside. Wearing gloves, carefully shake out the contents of each bag. What do you observe? Worms or other creepy crawlies? Mushrooms and other fungi? Sulphury smells? Which items show signs of biodegradation? How do the samples compare to the pictures you took two weeks ago?

❯ **Update your chart to fill in** "How accurate was my prediction?"

Try This!

Evoware, an environmentally friendly company in Jakarta, Indonesia, believes seaweed is the perfect raw material for biodegradable food packaging. Two-thirds of Indonesia's territory is water. It's one of the world's largest producers and exporters of seaweed. Packaging made from seaweed can dissolve in water or become edible food wraps.

A zero-waste food package you can eat! Watch this brief video about sustainable Evoware. How will the product minimize plastic waste?

🔎 YouTube edible package

WHIP UP AN EDIBLE LANDFILL

Follow the recipe to make your own landfill model! Have an adult help you with the oven.

20 graham crackers
2 tablespoons sugar
6 tablespoons butter
milk

2 boxes instant butterscotch pudding
8 fruit strip pieces
2 gingersnaps, crushed
10 thin pretzel sticks

¼ cup raisins
¼ cup nuts
chocolate sprinkles
green sprinkles

❯ **Imagine the pie pan is a newly dug landfill.** First, you're going to make a graham cracker crust that represents the protective clay layer. Place about 12 graham crackers into a bowl and squash them until you have 1½ cups.

❯ **Pour the crumbs into a mixing bowl and add the sugar.** Melt butter in a small bowl in the microwave and add it to the crumbs. Use a spatula to blend the ingredients. Then, press the dough all around the pie pan. Bake at 350 degrees Fahrenheit for 8 to 10 minutes and allow it to cool completely.

❯ **Follow directions on the pudding box to combine the mix and milk.** Set aside. Line the cooled crust with fruit strips. These are the landfill's soft plastic layer.

❯ **Flatten gingersnaps inside another bowl.** Scatter crumbs over the fruit strips. This is the gravel that holds down the plastic layer. Place pretzel sticks horizontally over the "gravel." These are pipes that collect water and methane gas.

❯ **Cover with a layer of pudding.** This represents food scraps and yard waste. Shake on raisins and nuts for reusable and recyclable bits and pieces.

❯ **Add another layer of pudding for more scrap and waste.** Add chocolate sprinkles to represent daily soil cover. Finally, drizzle on green sprinkles for grass!

Try This!

Watch the short film *The Landfill*, and discover how people are viewing trash in whole new ways.

🔎 Vimeo The Landfill

Chapter 4

HAZARDOUS
WASTE

I'M DONE ...EANING THE ...ASEMENT!

I JUST HAVE TO THROW THIS LAST BOX OF JUNK IN THE TRASH.

NICE! DID YOU KNOW THAT ...AZARDOUS WASTE ISN'T JUST OIL ...SPILLS AND INDUSTRIAL TOXINS.

MANY COMMON HOUSEHOLD ITEMS ARE HAZARDOUS WASTE...

...SUCH AS FURNITURE POLISH AND DRAIN CLEANER AND BUG SPRAY.

CAN YOU DO ME A FAVOR?

LOOK UP HOW TO SAFELY DISPOSE OF HOUSEHOLD HAZARDOUS WASTE?

YES, PLEASE.

Some trash is waste that harms people, animals, and the environment. Items that contain toxic and chemical materials sometimes make their way into our landfills. This harmful trash is called hazardous waste.

What does hazardous waste make you think of? Maybe it's toxic runoff that trickles from parking lots and splashes into rivers, or nasty **sewage** that floods beaches during heavy rains.

These are all good examples of hazardous waste. There are several other sources to be aware of as well. Let's take a look!

ESSENTIAL QUESTION

How does hazardous waste cause problems in landfills and the environment?

WORDS TO KNOW

sewage: waste from buildings, carried away through sewers.

catastrophic: involving or causing large amounts of damage.

refinery: factory where petroleum is separated into different oil types.

condensate: a poisonous liquid by-product of gas.

by-product: an extra and sometimes unexpected or unintended result of an action or process.

OIL SPILLS

Perhaps hazardous waste makes you think of **catastrophic** events. In April 2010, a British Petroleum (BP) oil rig called *Deepwater Horizon* exploded—11 people were killed. The devastating spill spewed 184 million gallons of crude oil into the Gulf of Mexico.

Can you visualize this much oil? According to the news group CNBC.com, it's enough to overflow 279 Olympic-sized swimming pools.

Warning sign of sewage on beach
credit: Tony Webster (CC BY 2.0)

Deepwater Horizon fire
credit: U.S. Coast Guard

The oil damaged ecosystems. It coated marine birds and animals. The spill also affected people who earn their livings by shrimping and fishing on the coast.

One problem created by the spill was where to put all the oil after it was cleaned up. Whenever possible, BP shipped reusable oil to **refineries**. Unfortunately, much of the oily waste wasn't recyclable, so BP had to put it into landfills in several Gulf Coast states.

Another spill happened in January 2018, when an enormous Iranian tanker collided with a Chinese grain freighter in the East China Sea, home of Asia's most bountiful fisheries. In the midst of this rich ecosystem, the tanker exploded into flames. All 32 crew members perished. About 1 million barrels of extremely flammable, poisonous **condensate**, a liquid **by-product** of gas, spilled into the sea and sank to the bottom.

Explore maps, graphics, and information about the negative ways the BP spill affected wildlife.

PS

🔎 NYT BP spill affects wildlife

The largest condensate spill in history, this impacted not only fish and the fishing industry, but also people who consume fish. When we eat fish, we eat whatever the fish has **ingested**, including toxins.

The spill's cleanup posed complex challenges, since the properties of toxic condensate differ from those of crude oil. Unlike the visible black slicks that spread after crude oil spills, which can be pumped out, condensate is nearly invisible.

The Keystone Pipeline Leak

Each day, the Keystone Pipeline carries nearly 600,000 barrels of crude oil from oil fields in Alberta, Canada, to oil refineries in Texas and Illinois in the United States. It passes through protected Native American lands, promised to the Great Sioux Nation in treaties, in Montana, South Dakota, Nebraska, Kansas, and Oklahoma.

In 2017, the pipeline leaked about 9,700 barrels of oil in rural Amherst, South Dakota, and seeped over rich farmlands. That's about 407,400 gallons of oil! In the aftermath, TransCanada Corp., the Calgary company that owns the pipeline, shut it down for repairs. During cleanup, 170 workers recovered almost 45,000 gallons of crude oil. They replaced contaminated topsoil and reseeded the area.

What caused the toxic underground leak? Investigators believe it was likely caused by mechanical damage to the pipe that occurred earlier, during construction in 2008. They feared other sections might also be faulty and at risk, which would threaten communities, water, and climate. In 2015, President Barack Obama denied the pipeline a permit for further construction. A federal judge upheld the decision in late 2018.

Some people in Houston had to be rescued by piggyback.
credit: Army National Guard photo by Lt. Zachary West

Sometimes, oil pollution can come from sources other than tanker ships. In 2017, massive Hurricane Harvey clobbered Houston, Texas. The nation's fourth-largest city is the center of the U.S. oil industry.

Houston boasts around 500 chemical plants, 10 refineries, and nearly 7,000 miles of mingled oil, gas, and chemical pipelines.

Read the article "The World Has Never Seen an Oil Spill Like This" from *The Atlantic.* Why is the condensate spill radically different from others? Research the spill. Locate satellite images, photos, and videos. Check progress on the cleanup. What's been accomplished? What's yet to be completed?

🔎 oil spill that wasn't Atlantic

During Harvey's onslaught, monster floods deluged the huge metropolitan area. Toxic substances, including benzene, butadiene, and vinyl chloride, were part of the industrial wastewater that spilled into Houston's neighborhoods. More than a year later, state and federal regulators remained unsure how many people would experience long-term health issues related to the devastation.

WORDS TO KNOW

ecopod: an ecologically friendly container.

UNDER THE KITCHEN SINK

Hazardous waste is pretty dangerous stuff, right? Yet most of us are right at home with products that produce hazardous waste. We handle them all the time. They're stashed under kitchen sinks and tucked in bathroom cabinets. They're tottering on shelves in garages and garden sheds!

For example, drain cleaners that dissolve goopy hairballs contain chemicals that can be toxic. So do furniture polish and window cleaner. You'll find toxins in sweet-smelling hair spray and stinky nail polish remover.

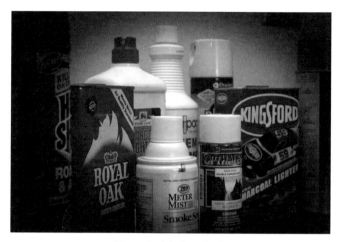

Household chemicals
credit: Official Marine Corps photo by Lance Cpl. Matthew K. Hacker

Even your dog's flea powder contains chemicals.

Upcycled Oil

If you know people who change their own motor oil, encourage them to recycle used oil at a service station or repair facility. According to the American Petroleum Institute, 2 gallons of recycled motor oil can generate enough electricity to power your house for 24 hours. Discarded oil from a single oil change pollutes 1 million gallons of fresh water. That's a year's water supply for 50 people—enough to fill 20,000 bathtubs!

Though we might not realize it, we frequently send toxic chemicals from household products out into the environment. We pour them down sinks, flush them down toilets, and spray them off driveways.

Imagine a bustling Saturday morning on your street. In the driveway, one neighbor scrubs the tires of a vintage Mustang with bubbly cleaner. Another neighbor sprays pesticide on prized roses, while a third refills windshield fluid in his car, spilling some onto the curb.

DID YOU KNOW?

Every year, enough hazardous waste is generated around the world to fill the New Orleans Superdome more than 1,500 times!

When it rains, toxic chemicals left behind from the bubbly cleaner, the pesticide, and windshield fluid mingle. They flow into the gutter. Eventually, these chemicals empty out into streams, lakes, and rivers, where they harm the environment.

Recycled Paper Caskets

Another source of toxic waste comes from graveyards and cemeteries. Death is a natural part of life. Even in death, people create garbage. How? It's not only bodies that are buried—caskets are, too. In the traditional burial industry, caskets are manufactured from hardwood, steel, and synthetic fabrics for shrouds and cushioning. When caskets are buried in cemeteries, they litter the planet underground.

The Natural Burial Company started in England and expanded to the United States and around the world. It's dedicated to sustainable, organic burial alternatives. The company makes burial **ecopods** out of biodegradable paper that breaks down in soil. These handmade caskets weigh about 40 pounds and can hold up to 210 pounds. Built of 100-percent recycled paper, including newsprint and printer paper, ecopods are covered in decorative wrapping made with mulberry bark.

WORDS TO KNOW

algae bloom: a rapid increase in an aquatic ecosystem's algae population.

medical waste: waste generated at hospitals and doctors' offices, such as needles, bandages, or blood.

DISPOSING OF HAZARDOUS HOUSEHOLD PRODUCTS

Household products that contain toxic chemicals require extremely careful handling. Paints, oils, and cleaners should be stored in a locked area away from people and pets, as the EPA recommends. Storing these products in this way also helps keep dangerous fumes out of your house.

You also must be careful when throwing away hazardous products. Try to use up materials such as paints or pass them along to someone who can finish them up. If they're dumped down drains, they'll pollute water supplies.

Tossed in the trash, hazardous waste will wind up in a landfill, where it mixes with leachate.

Find out when your community has a hazardous waste pick-up day. This is when toxic materials get hauled to special handling facilities.

Blooming!

In the early 2000s, runoff from dishwashers turned Washington State's Spokane River a gross shade of green! Why? Phosphates from dishwasher detergents promoted an **algae bloom**, which gave the river its green color. The algae used up all the oxygen in the water, creating an aquatic wasteland like a dead zone. In 2006, clean-water activists rallied for a statewide ban on household phosphates. They succeeded, and now the U.S. government has banned these phosphates for use in household products in all 50 states.

MEDICAL WASTE

Have you ever wondered where diseased lungs and gnarly warts wind up after doctors remove them? How about rotten teeth that dentists yank out or the needles the vet uses for your cat's shots?

All of these things become **medical waste**. Healthcare facilities, including hospitals, doctors' offices, and vets' clinics, all produce medical waste. By law, medical waste must be placed in special containers marked "Biohazard." Hazardous waste haulers remove the contents for safe disposal.

DID YOU KNOW?

Used to fill cavities, amalgam is a silver-colored mixture of mercury, tin, silver, copper, zinc, and other metals. Mercury is toxic and can cause mercury poisoning. Although generally considered safe for cavities, amalgam can't just be thrown out when it's old. Dentists must recycle it.

When not properly disposed of, medical waste threatens public health. In 2009, syringes and biohazard bags washed up on a New Jersey beach during the Fourth of July weekend. Beach patrols quickly herded swimmers out of the ocean before clearing away the toxic debris.

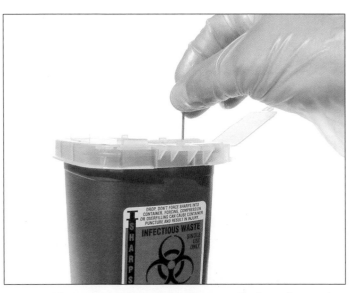

The proper way to throw out a medical needle
credit: William Rafti (CC BY 2.5)

RUBBISH WARRIORS

The Great Lakes are among our most precious **natural resources**. Sadly, much of the shoreline along these lakes is polluted. So, a group of Midwestern kids and teachers decided to do something about it.

They're part of the Alliance for the Great Lakes' Adopt-a-Beach program. Volunteers clean up littered beaches in Michigan, Minnesota, Ohio, and Wisconsin. In just one year, volunteers scooped up 186,000 soggy cigarette butts and cigar stubs!

Climate Change Corner

Away Is Here

In her blog post on NASA's Global Climate Change, author Laura Faye Tenenbaum writes, "As a society, we've become very selfish. People don't want to think about this big mound of trash. We want what we want and we don't care what happens to it after the trash truck drives off. Yup, that is us." However, she reminds us, "On Planet Earth, there is no 'away.' 'Away' is here."

As rubbish warriors, let's recognize and acknowledge the trash troubles most of us contribute to. How can communities protect "here"—our Earth—as we tackle waste? Tenenbaum writes about actions that reduce dependence on landfills and cut down on production of greenhouse emissions that cause climate change.

 Read the post to discover ways that waste-to-energy power plants convert trash to electricity.

🔍 NASA blog waste not

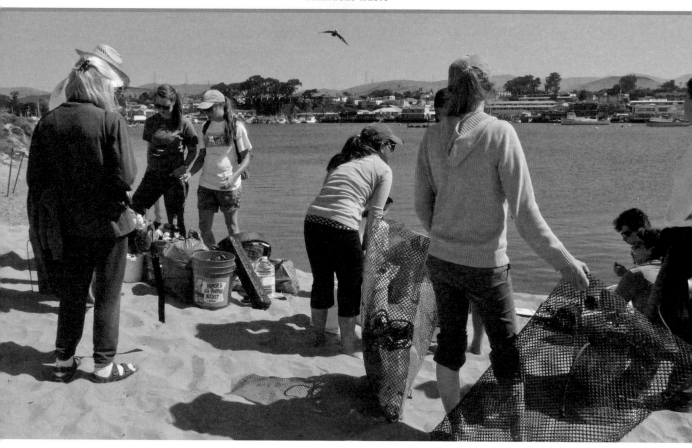

credit: Mike Baird (CC BY 2.0)

Groups of young people around the country are finding ways to be part of the rubbish solution. After a group of students in New York City pitched in to help clean up local beaches, they wrote to the Ocean Conservancy in Washington, DC, to share their observations. Jack, one of the kids, wrote, "I don't want to sound like I'm bossing people around, but you guys have to step up and get tough about this stuff."

Now that we've taken a look at some of the things that get thrown away and how they get disposed of, let's think about alternatives. You don't have to throw away something that you don't buy in the first place, right?

In the next chapter, we'll look deeper into the idea of reducing the amount of stuff we buy and therefore reducing the amount of waste we produce!

ESSENTIAL QUESTION

How does hazardous waste cause problems in landfills and the environment?

CLEAN UP AN OIL SPILL

Cleaning up an oil spill is extremely challenging. Water currents spread oil across waves and over beaches, which are nearly impossible to clean. When marine birds and mammals are "oiled," feathers and fur lose the protective coatings that make them waterproof. As they groom themselves, the bird and animals gulp down oil and die.

Sorbents are materials used to absorb liquids. Create an oil spill and test how different sorbents can clean it up. Then use feathers to simulate oiled birds. Use a scientific method worksheet to get organized.

❯ **Fill a clear plastic tub with clean water.** Depending on the tub's size, add 6–10 drops of blue food coloring. Mix in a teaspoon of salt and stir.

❯ **In a mixing bowl, combine ¾ cup of vegetable oil and 8 tablespoons of cocoa powder to represent crude oil.** You'll need to stir for quite a while to dissolve the oil and blend the ingredients.

❯ **Carefully pour the oil mixture into the tub of water.** Pour gently and slowly, or the simulation won't work. Observe whether the oil floats or sinks when you add it to water.

❯ **Gather sorbents to test, such as Brillo pads, paper towels, cotton balls, and rags.** Before you test the sorbents, predict which will be most successful in cleaning up the spill. Test each sorbent individually by carefully dipping it in the center of the water. What happens? Does the sorbent soak up the oil? The water? Does it float or sink? What conclusions can you draw?

Try This!

Add feathers to represent seabirds. Press the feathers into the water with a spoon and observe what happens. Do they float or sink? Add 2 or 3 squirts of dishwashing liquid to spread the oil. Use tweezers to remove the feathers. Wash the feathers with rags and paper towels. What happens?

WORDS TO KNOW

sorbent: a material that can absorb a liquid or semi-liquid.

COMPARE CLEANERS

What's lurking under your kitchen sink? Many common household cleaners are harmless, but others contain chemicals that could be hazardous. Can homemade, natural cleaning products work as effectively as commercial products? You be the judge! Get an adult's permission to do this project and wear rubber gloves. Use only the cleaners listed below.

❯ **Test a commercial glass cleaner such as Windex first.** Spray it onto a window and use rags or newspaper to wipe the surface. How well does the product work? What are its strengths and weaknesses?

❯ **Combine 1 quart warm water, ¼ cup inexpensive white or apple cider vinegar, and 2 tablespoons lemon juice for your natural cleaner.** Vinegar is a mild acid, and lemon juice is a citric acid that adds a clean, fresh scent. Pour the mixture into a spray bottle and test it on another glass surface. How does the homemade product compare with the commercial one? Record your results in your science notebook.

❯ **Select a wood table or cabinet to test a commercial furniture polish on.** What do you observe?

❯ **Combine ¾ cup inexpensive olive oil and ¼ teaspoon inexpensive white or apple cider vinegar in another spray bottle.** Test a tiny area of another surface to make sure the cleaner doesn't hurt the finish. Then, polish the surface. How does it compare with the commercial product? What conclusions can you draw about all the products? Record your results. **Hint:** These recipes contain items that spoil. Use up homemade cleaners on other glass and wood surfaces within a few weeks.

Try This!

Research do-it-yourself recipes for natural cleaning products. Using ingredients you have around the house, whip up your own cleaner.

WORDS TO KNOW

commercial product: a product produced in large quantities by business.

EXPERIMENT WITH DETERGENTS

When we dump detergents into the environment, they can have an impact on the way plants grow. In this two-week project, test household products to discover how plants respond. Be careful handling detergents and get an adult's permission to do this project.

❯ **Use three of the same plants of equal size in plastic containers,** such as beans, marigolds, and ivy.

❯ **Combine ¼ cup each of two different commercial detergents with ¼ cup of water in two glass jars with lids.** For example, use liquid laundry detergent and powdered dishwasher detergent. Label the jars.

❯ **Label the plant containers.** Write "Control" on one. Label the second with the name of one detergent and the third with the name of the other detergent. Start a scientific method worksheet. Measure the height of each plant and record it in your science journal. Add the date next to it.

❯ **Water the control plant with ¼ cup plain water.** Water the other two plants with the appropriate mixture. Place all three plants in a sunny location.

❯ **For two weeks, sprinkle the control plant with water every other day.** Sprinkle the other two plants with more detergent-and-water mixture. After two weeks, assess the results.

❯ **Measure each plant and compare the measurement with its starting height.** How did each plant do? What conclusions can you draw about the impact of detergents on plant growth?

Consider This!

What does this experiment show you about the effect of detergents in the water? How might grasslands, forests, rainforests, or other natural areas grow differently if they were exposed to this kind of chemical pollution?

Chapter 5

REDUCE

OKAY, YOU'VE CONVINCED ME. I'M DOING MY BEST TO PRODUCE LESS GARBAGE.

I DON'T WANT GARBAGE HEAVEN TO GET FULL.

WHAT'S GARBAGE HEAVEN?!

IT'S THE PLACE WHERE ALL THE GARBAGE GOES WHEN ITS TIME HERE IS DONE.

IT ENTERS THE WASTE STREAM THEN GOES TO A BETTER PLACE.

YOU KNOW THAT ALL THIS TRASH GOES TO THE LANDFILL, RIGHT?

OF COURSE, BUT IF I THINK OF IT AS GARBAGE HEAVEN, THEN I DON'T GET SO GROSSED OUT.

The future of Earth's environmental health doesn't have to be all doom and gloom. We can focus on opportunities for change and find new ways to use our valuable resources wisely.

The great news is that we're in charge of our choices and actions. We choose what to buy, how to use it, and how to dispose of it. We share this planet, and we can all pitch in to take care of our planet, now and for the future.

The first step is to reduce the amount of materials and products that we use. Reducing what we use preserves Earth's resources and cuts down the amount of garbage we send to landfills.

ESSENTIAL QUESTION

How will you precycle and reduce to limit what you dump into the waste stream?

In the first chapter, you discovered how much waste your family produces. Now it's time to reduce it!

SUSTAINABILITY

Have you heard people using the word **sustainability**? What does it mean?

Sustainability means living in a way that uses Earth's resources very carefully. We don't want these resources to run out, so we can't use them up without concern for the future.

In 2008, the World Wildlife Fund (WWF) issued an alarming report: "If our demands on the planet continue to increase at the same rate, by the mid-2030s we would need the equivalent of two planets to maintain our lifestyles." Two planets! And now, the 2030s are right around the corner.

Clearly, our way of life isn't sustainable. It devours Earth's resources without replacing them. Our lifestyle pollutes air and water. We bulldoze land to build landfills, then jam-pack them with our waste.

Simple Ways You Can Reduce

Add another R—refuse! Turn down packaging from the get-go and use **ingenuity** to figure out new solutions to old problems. Try some of these ideas!

› Put dinner leftovers in reusable containers for lunch the next day.

› Send electronic birthday party invitations instead of paper ones.

› Use non-breakable, reusable plates, cups, and silverware instead of paper or plastic for a picnic or when you have a group of friends over.

› Always have a reusable water bottle with you so you don't ever have to buy bottled water.

› Keep a reusable cup in the bathroom for rinsing after brushing instead of using disposable paper cups.

› Use a dishtowel instead of a paper towel to clean up spills.

› Buy loose fruits and veggies instead of packaged ones.

› When you need to buy packaged goods, buy only in recyclable packaging.

Earth provides everything we need to live—air, food, water, and warmth. Earth's gifts are a natural part of our lives. Sometimes, we take them for granted and expect them to always be available—especially **renewable** ones. Renewable resources such as water, timber, and fish can be replaced after we use them.

However, renewable doesn't mean never-ending.

What happens if we use up all the water in dry regions before it's replaced? Or chop down forests faster than they grow back? Or gobble up so much fish they don't have time to reproduce? Right now, we're **exhausting** our resources and failing to plan well for the future. Earth's resources are not unlimited.

WORDS TO KNOW

precycling: buying less and creating less waste.

So, what do we do about this? How can we change our habits, our ways of life, and our industries to ensure that future generations have the resources they need to thrive on this planet? Let's take a look.

PRECYCLE IT!

Are you **precycling**? The prefix "pre" means "before." Precycling is reducing waste by rethinking purchases and buying less stuff. Recycling is a good thing, but it takes resources to transport materials, melt them down, and then make new items. Precycling means less needs to get recycled in the first place.

What your family buys can have a tremendous impact on waste. For instance, you might buy a handy grab-and-go package of pizza for lunch. It comes in a cardboard box. Inside is a plastic tray and a plastic sheet. Mini crusts and shredded cheese fill compartments, along with a sauce pouch. There's a plastic bottle of water with a cap and a wrapped cookie for dessert.

Our natural resources are being used up at an alarming rate!

Tally all that packaging, and you rack up eight pieces of rubbish! And that's just your lunch. If you stop buying products such as this, you take an important step in reducing waste.

What choices can you make to avoid producing so many piece of trash for one meal?

Rethink grab-and-go. Plan ahead to reduce your reliance on processed and packaged foods. Get your chef's hat on and do it yourself!

For instance, make your own pizza at home with your family. Store a few leftover slices in reusable containers for your personal brand of grab-and-go. You don't even have to make the crust. Just buy dough, roll it out, and add toppings you like. It's easy! Not only do you drastically reduce waste and conserve energy, but you also enjoy incredible satisfaction. You made it yourself—with fresh ingredients.

Plus, it's healthier!

You can even make miniature pizzas using bagels or English muffins!

PACKAGING AND SOURCE REDUCTION

What was your favorite birthday present? Did it come in a box with lots of plastic inside and a set of instructions? Where was it made?

When manufacturers ship products long distances, they use extra packaging to keep the items from getting squashed. Transportation requires more fossil fuels that cannot be replaced. What did you do with the packaging? Throw it out? Keep it to reuse? Recycle it?

WORDS TO KNOW

source reduction: decreasing the quantity of waste, especially in packaging, so there is less to dispose of.

preventive: stopping something before it happens.

processed food: food that has added ingredients to make it look nicer, taste better, last longer, or cost less.

compostable: a material that can break down and rot in a compost heap.

Packaging is one of the largest contributors to our waste stream. That's why many manufacturers are working on **source reduction**. Source reduction means decreasing the amount of waste at the source, or beginning, of the waste stream. Fewer packing materials mean less to dispose of later.

Source reduction is **preventive**. It stops something from happening. In this case, it stops the production of garbage you have to get rid of later. When manufacturers make lighter plastic bottles or thinner straws that require less plastic, for example, they cut down the amount that becomes waste later.

How about buying in bulk?

Here, Have Some Junk!

Marketplace, a program about business and the economy, reports that American diets include 71 percent more **processed foods** than fresh food. Processed foods, which are canned, frozen, or dehydrated, are often loaded with salt, sugar, and chemicals. Have you ever checked out the ingredients listed on processed, prepackaged foods? Anything you recognize as real food, or are most ingredients very long words you can't pronounce? Not only are many processed foods unhealthy, they also come in lots more packaging than fresh foods.

With your family, listen to this episode of *Marketplace*. Discuss what you learned. How does your family's use of processed foods compare? Why do you think we're so dependent on processed foods?

🔎 Marketplace processed food

Buying in bulk means buying a larger container of something, which means you'll be buying less packaging. In some grocery stores, for example, you can scoop rice and flour out of bins and put it into reusable bags instead of buying a small package of rice or a small bag of flour. When you buy in bulk, you are cutting down on the amount of material that will need to be thrown away or recycled.

Another way to be part of the packaging solution is to not buy into the hype. Glitzy packages are fun and designed to grab your attention. They practically screech, "Pick me!" Yet, they usually cost more and don't add to the quality of what's inside.

When you can, buy items "bare," with no packaging at all. If that's not possible, try to buy products with certified **compostable** or recyclable packaging. Reuse packaging whenever you can. And who needs disposable packaging anyway when you can bottle homemade jams, bake your favorite muffins, and grow your own tomatoes for salsa?

What? I Can't Hear You Over the Chip Bag!

Have you eaten Sun Chips? These chips used to come in biodegradable bags made of plants. Consumers loved helping the environment while crunching on their favorite snack. But eco-friendly bags came with an unexpected twist. Noise pollution! Stiff bags produced a deafening racket and even inspired a Facebook page, "Sorry But I Can't Hear You Over This Sun Chips Bag." The Frito-Lay company decided to ditch the bags and go back to the drawing board. They added a rubber-based sticky substance to hold layers together. The new bags are quieter and still biodegradable. At least Frito-Lay could hear the complaints!

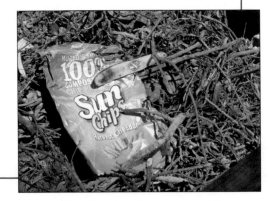

A Sun Chip bag in a compost pile
credit: Alan Levine (CC0 BY 1.0)

WORDS TO KNOW

crops: plants grown for food and other uses.

vermicomposting: using worms in compost to break down and recycle food wastes.

castings: rich, digested soil worms leave behind as waste.

gizzards: muscular organs in the digestive track.

IN THE GARDEN, NOT IN THE GARBAGE

When you toss organic waste into garbage cans, it ends up in a landfill. Organic waste produces methane, a greenhouse gas that contributes to global warming and climate change.

Why not try composting? Composting speeds up the breakdown of organic waste. It naturally decays with the help of decomposers and gives something back to the planet—a pesticide-free fertilizer.

Mandatory Food Scrap Recycling

Do you live in a city or state with mandatory food scrap recycling? In some places, laws require that organic waste be turned into compost. Mandatory composting makes an enormous difference. Food waste is eliminated from the waste stream! In 2009, the city of San Francisco in California passed the Mandatory Recycling and Composting Ordinance. By 2020, the city with a population of 870,000 wants to achieve an ambitious goal of zero waste. The San Francisco Department of the Environment wants all waste to be recycled or composted, with none dumped in landfills.

By law, people must separate trash into three color-coded bins—blue for recycling, green for composting, and black for landfill trash. Throughout the city, bins are labeled in English, Spanish, and Chinese.

Even if you're one of San Francisco's 25 million annual visitors, the law requires you to pitch in with residents and businesses. What happens to the nutrient-rich compost? It's sold to organic farmers and wine growers—who use it to cover **crops**.

So close the loop and practice another R—rot!

You can build a contained compost heap in a garbage can. Compost should contain three basic ingredients: greens, browns, and water. Green items, such as grass, contain nitrogen. Brown items, including dead leaves, are carbon-rich. They'll attract decomposers that hop to it and break down wastes. When you add water to organic materials, it helps them decay.

What if you don't have a yard or room for an outdoor compost? You can still reduce the amount of stuff you chuck in the trash. Bring it indoors with **vermicomposting**. Worms are stellar recyclers. They munch more than their own weight in garbage each day, digest it, and release waste called **castings**. Castings mingle with decaying organic materials and produce rich fertilizer.

Do you compost food scraps at your school? Many schools now have composting programs so kids can send their leftovers to a useful place instead of the landfill!

DID YOU KNOW?

Worms are toothless. Like birds, they use **gizzards**, muscular organs in the digestive tract, to crush and grind food.

THE LAST STRAW

In the United States alone, people use 500 million straws a day! That's enough straws to twist in a chain around the planet two and a half times—in just one day.

Those single-use plastic tubes you use for minutes to slurp down a drink probably come wrapped in a slip of plastic or paper. This makes a double-dose of plastic pollution that contributes to the enormous issue of waste.

Straws aren't biodegradable, and they're difficult to recycle.

Straw Bans

In 2018, Seattle, Washington, became the first major city in the United States to ban straws in restaurants and bars. Major corporations including Starbucks and Bon Appétit Management Company, which provides food service in businesses, college cafeterias, and museum cafes, announced future goals of eliminating single-use plastic straws. It was a solid step toward cutting waste and eliminating plastic pollution, and a challenge to discover compostable and recyclable alternatives.

However, without straws, many people would not be able to safely drink. For many, straws are necessary access tools. Advocates for disability rights and the elderly argue that banning bendy straws will be barriers for those who rely on them to consume liquids. Patients who recline in hospital beds depend on straws, too.

At this point, compostable straws don't have the same sturdiness as plastic ones. Flimsy compostable straws present choking hazards. To address the critical issue, Seattle passed its straw ban with an exemption. It allows businesses to provide bendy plastic straws to customers with physical or medical conditions.

Mounds and mounds of straws are commonly dumped at picnic areas, parks, and beaches, where the wind scatters them. When straws inevitably make their way to our oceans, they pollute water. Turtles and other marine wildlife mistake them for food.

RUBBISH WARRIOR

DID YOU KNOW?

A staggering 71 percent of seabirds and 30 percent of turtles have been discovered with plastics in their bellies.

When Milo Cress from Burlington, Vermont, was nine years old, he launched a program to battle that gigantic number of straws. He created the Be Straw Free Campaign and appealed to local restaurants and decision-makers. Then he headed to Washington, DC, to speak to the House and Senate and challenge others to skip the straw.

Milo knows even small steps protect our planet's future. At age 16, he told the *Washington Post*, "My favorite part about it has been getting to talk to other kids and listening to their ideas. It's really cool, and I think it's really empowering. I certainly feel like I'm listened to and valued in a larger community, and I really appreciate that."

Help attack tremendous waste. Get sucked in. Skip the straw! Swap reusable stainless steel, glass, or bamboo straws for plastic.

ESSENTIAL QUESTION

How will you precycle and reduce to limit what you dump into the waste stream?

PS **With family and friends, watch the video *The Last Straw.*** How does Milo inspire you to take action and develop waste-reducing strategies of your own?

🔎 young voices last straw

BUILD A GARBAGE CAN COMPOST HEAP

Try composting greens and browns to reduce waste. Greens include fruit and veggie scraps, coffee filters and grounds, eggshells, grass clippings, and teabags. Browns are autumn leaves, bark, branches, hay, straw, and twigs. You will want to wear gardening gloves.

Caution: Do not compost any meat, bones, or fish.

❯ **Scout around to find an ideal location for your heap.** Make sure it's in a protected, shady place not too close to your house. If it's too close, critters attracted to the heap might get into your house. Use a large plastic garbage can with holes punched or drilled several inches up from the bottom. Arrange bricks, a pallet, or 2-by-4-inch pieces of lumber as a foundation for the garbage can. Place the can on top.

❯ **Compost needs a balanced diet.** Put on gloves and divide green and brown materials into piles of equal size. Break, chop, or shred larger chunks of materials. First, spread a 6-inch layer of browns in the can. Then spread a 3-inch layer of greens on top of the browns. Add several handfuls of soil over the greens. Use your hands or a shovel to carefully mix layers.

❯ **Add another 3-inch layer of greens and more soil.** With a garden hose, wet but don't drown the heap. As a rule of thumb, keep the heap as wet as a damp sponge. Close the lid tightly and use rope or a bungee cord to secure it. That will keep hungry animals from scavenging.

DID YOU KNOW?

What keeps a lot of us from composting? The ick factor! When you throw food scraps into a garbage can, they're out of sight, out of mind. With composting, not so much. You get down and dirty. It takes time. And garden gloves work wonders. If you just can't get beyond the ick factor, find out if your community provides food scrap containers and curbside pickup for composting.

❯ **Get rolling! Your heap needs air and water to thrive.** Once a week, place the garbage can on its side and roll it like a barrel to mix the layers. Check to make sure the heap is moist. As bacteria break down waste, they produce heat, so you'll notice the compost warms up.

❯ **Once the heap is up and running, regularly add green and brown organic waste** to keep the compost cooking. Add some soil each time and keep it moist.

❯ **Depending on where you live and what the surrounding conditions are like, it will take between one and six months for your compost to cook.** When it's ready, the materials will look like rich, dark soil—black gold! You're ready to spread your all-natural fertilizer in flowerbeds or use it for outdoor potting soil.

Try This!

It will take trial and error to discover the ideal mix of greens and browns. Equal parts might not work for you. If not, then vary the ratio. Try three parts browns to one part greens and observe the results.

Composting In Schools

Does your school compost leftover food scraps instead of pitching them out and away to a landfill? In school cafeterias, food waste and paper napkins can be separated from landfill trash and recyclables. In the state of Wisconsin, Compost Crusader is an organics recycling company. Compost Crusader works with schools to keep food scraps out of landfills. Separation starts at the source—the lunchroom. After eating, kids presort waste and recyclables at lunch tables. They take turns manning waste stations to help others. Everyone pitches in to pour leftover liquids into a slop bucket and divide other wastes into color-coded containers. Then, Compost Crusader hauls organic wastes to a commercial site, where it's mixed with yard waste. In time, the waste becomes nutrient-rich compost.

BECOME A WORM FARMER

Red wigglers work best in this worm farm! Find them in at a bait store or worm farm.

Hint: Don't use earthworms. They can't work on this farm, since they need a much deeper space to survive.

Include on the worm menu

- small amounts of coffee grounds
- thoroughly crushed eggshells
- fruit and veggie peels and scraps
- teabags (remove metal staples or attachments) and tea leaves

Don't feed worms

- animal waste
- bones
- butter or oils
- egg yolks or whites
- fish or meat

❯ **Use a small, non-transparent plastic storage tub or organizer box with a lid**—worms like things dark, so if you only have a see-through container, cover the outside with black construction paper to block out light. Your worm farm needs good air circulation. Ask an adult to drill or punch several holes in the bottom and top of your container for drainage and air.

credit: allispossible.org.uk (CC BY 2.0)

❯ **Make cozy, edible bedding for the worms.** Use your hands to shred black-and-white newspaper into 1-inch strips. Colored or glossy pages can harm worms, so don't use those! Fill the container about halfway with fluffed-up newspaper. Spritz the bedding with water, but don't make it too soggy. Worms need moisture, but they'll die if conditions are too wet. Too much humidity might also invite pesky fruit flies.

❯ **Add 2 cups of soil to the bedding.** Use your hands to thoroughly mix the soil into the newspaper. Then gently place red wrigglers into the bedding. Worms love dark spaces, so give them time to burrow away from the light and into the bedding.

❯ **Once the worms burrow into a cozy spot, layer food scraps onto the bedding.** Scraps might include fruit and veggie leftovers, coffee grounds, crushed eggshells, teabags, and tea leaves. The smaller the pieces, the easier it is for worms to work their wonders, so chop or break up the materials. Add another fluffy layer of newspaper on top to fend off yucky odors.

❯ **Worms thrive in temperatures between 55 and 75 degrees Fahrenheit,** so put your farm in a shady, cool place away from direct sunlight. A basement, laundry room or kitchen corner works well. A garage is great, too. Because there are holes in the bottom of the farm, it will drain. Place the farm on top of bricks or wooden blocks with a tray underneath to collect drainage, called compost tea. The tea makes a nutritious treat for houseplants, so slip them a sip.

❯ **Check in with the worm farm every day.** Make sure the bedding stays slightly moist. Add more food scraps. Over a period of about 3 to 6 months, worms will churn out rich compost. When it's time to remove the crumbly compost, coax the wrigglers to one side of the container. If you place some food in one area, the worms will wriggle to that spot. It might take a couple of days. Carefully scoop out compost from the other side. Add new bedding—and let the recycling continue.

DID YOU KNOW? Red wigglers live in colonies. They are active at night, when it's time to eat. During chow time, worms wriggle together in a close mass around food sources.

Try This!

It takes trial and error to keep the farm thriving. You might need to increase or decrease moisture or move the farm to a warmer or cooler location. Trust your powers of observation and keep trying.

GROW AN AVOCADO PLANT

Holy guacamole! Don't pitch that pit. Let it live on in a new plant.

❯ **Under cool running water, wash the pit to remove bits of avocado clinging to it.** Gently blot it dry. Then, turn the pit so the wider end faces down and the pointy end is up. Carefully push toothpicks into the pit, sticking one toothpick on each of the four sides.

❯ **Hang the avocado over the rim of a glass of water.** Make sure there's enough water in the glass to submerge the pit about halfway.

❯ **Place the glass in a warm, sunny location and check it every day.** As the water level goes down, add more fresh water. After about a week, the pit's brown layer will probably peel off and break away. In about two or three weeks, a root nub will pop from the bottom, and the pit will gradually split open. After about six weeks, a thin stem will spring from the upper part. In time, leaves will roll out from the stem.

Avocado pits for sprouting

❯ **When the leaves are about an inch long, you're ready to transplant.** Fill a clay pot or planter with potting soil. Remove the toothpicks and bury the roots and pit in the soil. Keep your plant in a sunny location and water it regularly so the soil stays moist.

❯ **Avocado plants tend to get leggy.** For a fuller plant, prune back the stem by snipping it with scissors when it gets to be about 4 inches high.

❯ **Move your potted avocado plant outdoors in warm weather.** Depending on what kind of climate you live in, you might be able to transplant it into the ground and grow a tree!

Try This!

Grow a sweet potato vine using the same directions. Instead of a glass, use a large jar filled with water and extra toothpicks if needed.

Chapter 6

REUSE

So many products are at our disposal in a throwaway world. Diapers, tiny packets of mustard, paper towels—they're designed to be used once for convenience and then tossed out. We ditch the old to make way for the new. We dump broken things instead of fixing them.

It can be easy to fall into throwaway thinking. But you don't have to be part of a throwaway world. Learn to reuse. This means saving things instead of throwing them out. And then finding new (and sometimes better!) ways to use them. You're not only keeping items from entering the waste stream, but you're also using creativity and ingenuity.

Be **innovative**! Challenge yourself to consider stuff in whole new ways. What are alternatives to throwing things out? One option is to reuse items, even some disposable ones, in their original state.

SSENTIAL QUESTION

Iow can you use
reativity and ingenuity
o reuse items?

For example, if you use plastic plates, cups, and forks on a family outing, make them last. Wash and reuse them for the next picnic or camping trip. Wash Ziploc bags repeatedly and air-dry them on racks.

Instead of chucking broken items, fix them so they're better than ever. Repair rickety skateboards. Patch flat tires on your bike. Condition a dried-up baseball glove.

Devise clever ways to repurpose stuff.

This means taking old things and using them for something they weren't originally made for. For example, use empty glass jars from jams and nut butters to store dried beans, pasta, or oats. Make quirky storage baskets from faded blue jeans. Wrap funky fabric scraps around wooden bracelets to dress them up. Instead of rolling an old tire into a landfill, use it for a tree swing.

DID YOU KNOW?

What materials can you cobble together to build your own usable furniture—without buying anything?

From Trash to Treasure

Nelson Molina, who worked as a sanitation worker in East Harlem, New York, for more than 30 years, has rescued an amazing array of treasures bound for the landfill. Molina's "pickings" include antique stained glass, busted violins, signed baseballs, military memorabilia, university diplomas, and much, much more.

Visit *Hyperallergic*, the online arts magazine, to explore the astonishing Treasures in the Trash Museum in New York City! What surprises you about the discarded items? What stories do they hint at?

🔎 Hyperallergic trash

Find a Repurpose!

Try these easy ideas for repurposing things instead of throwing them away!

> Use old sheets and quilts for picnic blankets.

> Scrub an old cutting board with half a lemon to refinish it.

> Screw vintage drawer pulls onto a chunk of wood to make a jewelry hanger.

> Mount dresser drawers on the walls to make bookshelves.

> When it's time to replace a door, use the old one to make a desk or drawing table.

> Turn an old sink or even a bathtub into a backyard planter.

> Create a tote bag from a pillowcase.

> Convert old shutters to a bulletin board and tuck notes between the slats.

WORDS TO KNOW

upcycle: to remake old products into something more environmentally friendly, and often of better quality and value.

Another way to reuse items is to donate to charitable organizations such as Goodwill, The Salvation Army, and veterans' groups in your community. Give magazines, books, and DVDs to nursing homes, shelters, and libraries. Find out if there's a Habitat for Humanity ReStore in your area. These resale shops accept gently used furniture, appliances, and building materials.

UPCYCLE

Rummage through vintage, thrift, and consignment shops. Scout out garage and yard sales. Trade clothes with friends. Then, give **upcycling** a whirl!

Upcycling is different from recycling, which breaks down materials. And it's different from repurposing, because when you upcycle, you take old materials and turn them into something not just different, but new and better.

For example, find old clothes in a thrift shop and make them into unique fashions. Cut arms off a coat to create a vest and decorate it with old buttons and beads. Design a kimono using a colorful silk scarf.

Sometimes it seems like an endless stream of stuff flows into our homes. Don't just throw it out to a landfill when you're done with it. Remember, many items can be rescued and improved.

Tips for Upcycling

> Cut up an old vinyl or oilcloth tablecloth and make stylish lunch bags out of the pieces.

> Use sweater sleeves to make fingerless gloves, and use the rest of the material to make a sweater for your dog.

> Snip wallpaper scraps and notebook paper to make miniature journals.

> Connect old watch faces to make a bracelet.

> Grow a terrarium inside an old lighting fixture.

> Clean a yogurt container and cover it with fabric scraps and beads to make a gift box.

> Use colorful paint to jazz up an old accent table or chair.

> Use fabric paint on old canvas shoes to give them a new look.

> Glue old table legs to a suitcase to craft a storage table.

> Create mosaics with broken china and pottery or pieces of leftover tile.

> Craft a birdfeeder from a 2-liter plastic bottle and thin dowel rods for perches.

RUBBISH WARRIORS

Kids battled waste and changed their world! They helped build a new school with sustainable infrastructure, And they used materials easily and inexpensively available—discarded plastic bottles.

More than 1,800 kids from the rural region around Sepalua, Guatemala, joined together with dedication and ingenuity to clean up their communities.

Working with community organizers, they gathered and stuffed 2.5 tons of inorganic garbage into more than 10,000 plastic bottles to make "eco-bricks." With frames constructed of concrete, metal, and chicken wire, community workers reused the bottles and constructed a new school.

Boy with eco-bricks
credit: Josephine Chan and Ian Christie (CC BY 4.0)

A typical bottle school takes about three months to build. Eco-bricks are not only cheaper than hollow concrete bricks, but they are also nearly three times stronger. Bottle schools are much more than buildings with four walls. They are symbols of kids acting and building a brighter future for themselves and the planet.

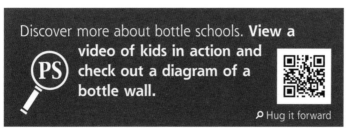

Discover more about bottle schools. **View a video of kids in action and check out a diagram of a bottle wall.**

🔍 Hug it forward

ESSENTIAL QUESTION

How can you use creativity and ingenuity to reuse items?

ENDS PICTURE FRAME

What's wasting away in your junk drawers? In this project, you'll decorate a picture frame with thingamajigs and doodads.

❱ **Find a wood or plastic picture frame to reuse.** Gather odds and ends and found objects such as shells, acorns, broken toys and jewelry, foreign coins, and boardgame pieces. If you'd like, include optional decorations such as glitter, sequins, and beads. **Hint:** Don't have a frame? Build your own out of old cardboard or glue together used Popsicle sticks.

❱ **Examine your objects.** Do you notice a theme or pattern in your stuff? Or is it random? Decide how you want items to be arranged on your frame and glue them on.

❱ **Place the frame on newspaper to dry overnight.** Make sure the decorated side is facing up. Check on the frame now and then. If any doodads have slipped out of place, nudge them back to where they belong. Add more glue if needed.

❱ **When the frame has thoroughly dried, carefully peel away any glue drippings.** Add a picture.

DID YOU KNOW?

Sticky notes, napkins, printer paper. How much paper do you use each year? According to the EPA, if you're like the average American, it takes a 100-foot-tall Douglas fir tree to make enough paper for you for one year! What changes will you make to reduce that amount?

Try This!

Create frames to give as presents to your friends. What are they interested in? Sports? Animals? Theater? Find objects to glue onto your frames that reflect what your friends like to do.

JUNK MAIL BEAD NECKLACE

It's fun to get a card or package in the mail. But junk mail? Not so much. You don't ask for junk mail, but it shows up anyway. It's usually advertising materials such as catalogs, flyers, credit card applications, and even CDs. One credit card company sends out materials in a fancy gold box with a plastic window, two Styrofoam bumpers, and five individual flyers inside!

According to the New York University School of Law, most families in the United States receive 848 pieces of junk mail annually. About 46 percent is never even opened. Many people toss it straight into the trash, so about 5.6 million tons of the stuff clogs landfills.

Reuse junk mail to create colorful trash-to-treasure paper beads for a necklace.

Hint: Reuse clasps from broken jewelry. You can also string pearls, beads, and charms along with your completed paper beads.

❯ **Collect all the mail your family receives for one week.** Make one pile of regular mail and one of junk mail. Tally the number of pieces in each, and record your totals in your science journal. Weigh each pile and jot down those totals. How do they compare?

❯ **Place the junk mail into categories of your choice.** For example, make piles of catalogs, advertisements, flyers, or magazine subscription offers. How many pieces are in each pile? Note your findings.

❯ **Now it's time to reuse!** First decide how long you'd like your necklace to be. Measure a length of thin cord or fishing line and cut it.

❯ **Create a template with a piece of cardboard.** Draw a triangular shape 1 inch wide at its base and 6 inches long. Cut out the template and use it to trace about 30 strips on glossy paper from your junk mail. Cut out the strips. If you discover later that you need more beads, then come back to this step.

❯ **Firmly wrap the wide end of the first strip around a wooden skewer or chopstick and roll the strip toward the pointed end.** The tighter the paper, the more decorative the bead. When you have about 2 inches of bead left to roll, use a glue stick to swipe the remaining length.

❯ **Finish rolling the bead and hold it firmly in place until the glue sets.** Carefully remove the bead from the stick and set aside. Repeat with all the strips until you've made all the beads.

❯ **For strong, durable beads, seal them with a coat of decoupage glue, or Elmer's glue with water added.** This makes a nice finish. You might find

credit: Kate Lilley (CC BY 2.0)

it's easier to apply glue if you place each bead back on the skewer tip first. After applying the glue, set each bead aside to dry.

❯ **Tightly tie a metal clasp to an end of the fishing line.** When the beads are dried and feel firm to the touch, string them on the line. Once the line is completely full, tightly attach the other clasp. Enjoy your junk mail jewelry!

Try This!

Remove your names and address from junk mailing lists. To keep junk mail from showing up, go to the website for the Direct Marketing Association.

🔎 DMAchoice

STASH-IT LOCKER POCKET

Reuse old jeans to make a stash-it pocket for your locker or fridge.

❯ **Work with an old pair of jeans that have a pocket without rips or tears.** Snip away the pocket and piece of pants it's stitched onto. Cut as close to the pocket's fabric edge as you can.

❯ **Spread out newspaper as a drop cloth.** Use fabric paint to decorate the pocket. Allow the paint to dry completely.

❯ **When the paint has dried, glue on whatever embellishments you'd like,** such as sequins, beads, charms, ribbons, or something else. Let the glue dry completely.

DID YOU KNOW?

How do blue jeans get their distinctive color? With indigo dye, an organic compound that's been around since ancient times!

❯ **Flip over the pocket.** Use four magnetic strips. If the strips have peel-away covers, remove them and position two strips on the pocket sides and the other two on the top and bottom. Otherwise, glue the strips in place.

❯ **Stick your stash-it pocket inside your school locker or on your fridge.** Use it to hold pens, pencils, and other odds and ends.

Try This!

Research do-it-yourself projects to discover other ways to reuse, repurpose, or upcycle old jeans.

WORDS TO KNOW

embellishment: decoration, trimming.

MUSICAL WIND CHIMES

Do you have spoons that have been mangled in the garbage disposal? Don't chuck them! Reuse them to help make a melodious wind chime. You can later add other items such as as soda cans or metal pie plates.

❯ **Use one large serving fork, four metal spoons, and one regular fork with four tines.** Ask an adult to drill a hole at the end of each spoon and the fork. Flatten the spoons with a hammer.

❯ **Use pliers to bend each of the serving fork's tines.** First, bend outer tines out to the sides. Then, bend one inner tine backward and the other forward.

❯ **Cut a 12-inch piece of fishing line.** Thread one end through one spoon and securely knot it. Tightly tie the free end to one tine of the serving fork. Repeat with the other spoons. Need an extra set of hands? Ask someone to help you keep the lines from crossing and tangling.

❯ **Cut a final piece of line, about 22 to 24 inches long.** String it through the hole in the serving fork and tie a secure loop at the end. Hang your wind chime from a tree.

Consider This!

Today, if you go to a craft fair or an art gallery, you are likely to see art that was either inspired by the environment or that uses repurposed materials as a way to help the environment. Why do you think there's such a strong connection between art and the environment?

WORDS TO KNOW

tine: a point.

MILK JUG MR. BONES

"The back bone's connected to the neck bone. The neck bone's connected to the head bone." Have you ever heard the traditional tune "Dry Bones?" In this project, you'll reuse plastic milk jugs to connect bones on your own skeleton!

Caution: Have an adult help you with the cutting and the glue gun.

Hint: Depending on how you make your cuts, you might use fewer or more jugs.

❯ **Peel or soak off the labels on 12 washed plastic gallon milk jugs.** Start at the top of the skeleton, with Mr. Bones' skull. Not all gallon milk jugs look the same, so try to find one that has two round grooves on the side opposite the handle. Those hollowed out circles are the skull's eye sockets. Face the handle away from you and turn the jug upside down.

❯ **You're ready to make a skull face.** Use a marker to draw a skull's nose and wide, toothy grin. Ask an adult to help you use an X-Acto or craft knife. Cut out the eyes, nose, and mouth. Then, cut two ¼-inch slits at the top of the skull. Snip a long piece of string. Thread it through the slits and knot it securely so the completed skeleton can dangle from it.

❯ **Use another jug. Keep it right side up and turn the handle away from you.** Visualize a chest and ribcage. There's an area in the center of the jug that juts out. On each side of it, draw four rib bones. Slice through the plastic and cut out sections to complete the ribcage.

❯ **Join the skull and chest with a neck by using a glue gun to attach the spouts of the two jugs.** Hold the jugs firmly in place as the glue sets and cools.

❯ **For shoulders, cut off the handles of two more jugs.** Make sure you leave a curved section of plastic at the ends to attach arms later. Punch a hole at the end of each shoulder. Glue the other ends of the shoulders at the sides of the chest, with punched areas facing out.

▶ **Stand a jug on a flat surface to build hips.** Measure 4½ inches up from the base of the jug. Mark it with a horizontal line. Along the line, cut completely around the jug. Stand the smaller bottom piece you cut away on the table. In each of its four sections, snip out a half-moon shape. Choose two opposite corners and punch holes in each. Place the hips aside for now.

▶ **Ready for the waist?** Cut out two bottle spouts, making sure you leave a half-inch section of plastic around the bottom of each. Glue together the spouts' narrow ends. Glue the chest and hips to the dried waist. Hold firmly in place as the glue sets.

▶ **Use three jugs to make eight bones for arms and legs.** First, cut into the corner, contoured sections of the jugs to make four bones for the tops of arms and legs.

▶ **Cut away the center area of the jugs to make the other four bones.** They'll become lower arms and legs. Punch holes through both ends of all the bones. Use string to connect both sets of arm bones. Tie arms to the shoulders. Use more string to connect both sets of leg bones. Tie those to the hips.

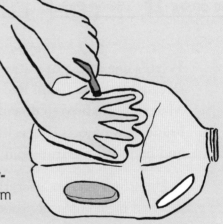

▶ **Trace your hands and bare feet on four of the remaining sides of jugs.** Cut them out, and punch holes where wrists and ankles will connect to arms and legs. Tie them to the skeleton.

▶ **For an eerie touch, coat Mr. Bones with glow-in-the-dark paint.** After your skeleton dries, hang him outside and let him rattle his bones in the breeze.

Try This!

Using milk jugs and your imagination, design and build your own Halloween decorations. Make kooky masks, scary ghosts, or Frankenstein monsters.

Chapter 7

RECYCLE

What's one of the best ways to prevent items from entering the waste stream? Recycle them! Recycling is a loop, or continuous process. Materials are broken down, then built back up again and used to create brand-new objects. Recycling conserves natural resources, saves energy, and helps the environment.

Unfortunately, not everything can be recycled. Materials that can be recycled include plastic, paper, glass, and metal. Recycled materials are used to make more of the same item or create brand-new products.

Your family probably recycles now. Do you help? You can pitch in by separating recyclables from trash. Bottles, jars, newspapers, junk mail, and even flat tires can be recycled into new products.

ESSENTIAL QUESTION

How will you challenge yourself to recycle more?

Take recyclables to a recycling center or lug them to the curb for pickup so they enter the recycling stream. Instead of heading to landfills, recyclables temporarily move to a transfer station or materials recovery plant. At the plant, workers clean, dry, and sort materials before they move along to be **reprocessed**.

WORDS TO KNOW

reprocess: to break down, treat, and prepare to recover materials to use again.

How are materials separated?

Mega magnets snatch metals off conveyer belts. Hand sorters stand along belts and yank out plastics, cardboard, paper, and glass. They separate plastics by identification codes, divide paper into various types, and organize glass according to color.

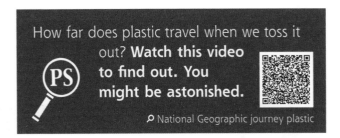

How far does plastic travel when we toss it out? **Watch this video to find out. You might be astonished.**

PS

⌕ National Geographic journey plastic

Recycling Bins

Drink cans

Glass & Plastic Bottles

Paper

After everything has been separated, it goes to the reprocessing plant. This is where materials are broken down. Workers at these plants shred plastics, reduce paper to pulp, crush glass, and melt metals. Broken-down plastic, paper, and glass get tightly bundled into bales. Meanwhile, melted metal is poured and shaped into bars or blocks.

Garbage goals! Sweden's recycling program is so epic, the country ran out of trash! **Read this article to discover how they accomplished it.**

PS

🔎 Sweden out of rubbish

Now these materials are ready to be sold to manufacturers, who use them to produce new items.

What Is Recycled?

› Materials used to make soft drink, sports drink, and salad dressing bottles can be recycled into new bottles. They can also be transformed into entirely new products, such as fleece clothing, carpeting, and even luggage.

› Shampoo bottles, yogurt tubs, and cereal boxes can be recycled into pipes, rope, doghouses, and recycling bins.

› Blood bags, medical tubing, and window frames can be recycled into new packaging, gutters, mud flaps, and traffic cones.

› Dry cleaning bags, frozen food bags, and squeezy mustard bottles can be recycled into compost bins, trash cans, and furniture.

› Ketchup and medicine bottles, as well as disposable diapers, can be recycled into traffic lights, bike racks, and rakes.

› CD cases, egg cartons, and disposable utensils can be recycled into new egg cartons, switch plate covers, and thermometers.

Recycling bales
credit: Michal Ma as (CC BY 3.0)

SHRINKING MARKETS FOR RECYCLED MATERIAL

The value of recovered waste products steadily nose-dived in the last few years. The recovery industry is limping along, struggling to gain profits.

Rob Taylor works for the State Recycling Program in the North Carolina Department of Environmental Quality. Taylor conducted a study. He learned that North Carolina's mixed recyclables in a recovery facility experienced a major drop in market value. Value plummeted from $180 a ton in 2011 to just $80 a ton in 2015.

DID YOU KNOW?

Greenphone.com pays you to recycle your old cell phone. The company figures out the trade-in value and sends you a check in that amount. The shipping cost is on them, too. The best news? Greenphone passes repurposed phones to people in need and plants a tree for every device recycled.

The value of recycled glass has particularly plunged. In fact, you might live in a community that has stopped collecting household glass in curbside recycling. What's causing the decline in profits? One key factor is the cost. It's so expensive to collect, separate, and ship waste materials for recycling that profits are minimal.

WORDS TO KNOW

obsolescence: uselessness.

e-waste: discarded electronics.

When we purchase recyclable and recycled products, we help close the loop.

This means Earth's natural resources don't get used up. And that means more clean air, soil, and water for the future. So, when you're making a purchase, try to buy flip-flops fashioned from shredded plastics or string beads crafted from crushed glass.

How much trash are you recycling? According to the Clean Air Council, folks in the United States recycle only about one-tenth of their solid garbage. Pitch in to boost that percentage. Not sure which items your community accepts for recycling? Do online research or pop in at your town hall to find out. Make sure you have recycling bins at home that everyone can get to easily.

In the United States alone, people use nearly 53 billion plastic water bottles a year. If you're like the average American, you use approximately 167 plastic bottles yearly—but only recycle 38 of them. **Watch this DNews video about recycling plastic bottles.** What happens when bottles aren't recycled? How does the process of recycling work? Now, commit to recycling your bottles whenever possible.

PS

𝒫 DNews does recycling help

That's Tricky

Isn't it annoying when electronics go kaput a few days after the warranty expires or the latest update crashes your old system? Blame it on something called planned **obsolescence**. Many people believe that products are designed to break down after a certain amount of time. Why? So we'll have to buy new ones! Not only do companies make more money if people buy new versions of old products, there is a sharp consumer hunger for the latest and greatest device. Humans like to try new things. This might be good for business, but it's bad for the environment.

ELECTRONIC WASTE

How many electronic gadgets and gizmos do you have? The average American household uses 25, including three smartphones. Other electronic devices might be smart cameras, audio equipment, laptops, game systems, and TVs. And we're constantly upgrading as new models burst onto the market.

DID YOU KNOW?

If your household recycles newspapers every day for a year, you'll save five trees!

According to the United Nations Environmental Program, by the year 2021, people around the world will trash more than 52.5 million metric tons of electronic devices every year! In fact, the United Nations warns, "The growing volume of electronic waste, including discarded products with a battery or plug, such as mobile phones, laptops, televisions, refrigerators and electrical toys, poses a major threat to the environment and human health."

E-waste, or electronic waste, is the fastest-growing category of waste in the United States.

E-waste is hazardous because it contains arsenic, lead, and mercury. And you know what happens when hazardous waste gets squished into landfills: It becomes part of the garbage soup that leaks through and contaminates groundwater and soil.

Want to see the longest-burning lightbulb? The Centennial Bulb was first turn on 117 years ago in a fire station in Livermore, California—and it's still burning! **You can see it at this** webcam.

PS

🔎 centennial bulb webcam

To prevent this from happening, many communities provide ways to recycle this waste. E-waste recovery centers take apart electronics. They keep bits of copper wire, gold, and platinum that can be used again. Some places work to refurbish electronic devices to give them new life. That way, instead of heading to a landfill, they head to someone else's house to be useful for a while longer.

Gold, silver, bronze! What do Olympic medals have to do with e-waste? A lot! A company in Vancouver, Canada, made the 2010 Winter Olympic medals from metals recovered from old computer monitors, laptops, and printers.

Right now, the United States does not have federal regulations for handling e-waste. So what can you do? One solution is to research the way your community handles e-waste recycling. **Try to find a certified recycling center by visiting eStewards.**

PS

🔍 eStewards recyclers

E-waste
credit: Curtis Palmer (CC BY 2.0)

More Olympic organizers plan to do the same. The Olympic committee placed collection boxes throughout the city and invited people to pitch outdated electronics.

Some companies ship e-waste away. They send it out of sight and out of mind. But it goes somewhere. For example, some of our old computers and cell phones end up in dumps in places such as India and Ghana.

DID YOU KNOW?

A lot of our e-waste ends up in countries without strict environmental laws.

Recycled Vision

A girl squints at her baby brother's blurry face. A boy struggles in reading class, unable to make out words in his book. All around the world, people need glasses. Yet, every year in North America, we throw out 4 million pairs of eyeglasses! Instead, you can give the gift of sight. Encourage your family and friends to recycle old glasses. Donate them to the Lions Club in your community. Many Lions Clubs place convenient drop-off boxes in libraries, schools, and eye doctors' offices. Find out where your nearest recycling center is located at this website.

Lions Club recycle eyeglasses

You can also mail eyeglasses in padded envelopes or boxes (try to reuse some packaging) to:

> Lions Clubs International Headquarters
> Attention: Receiving Department
> 300 W. 22nd Street
> Oak Brook, IL 60523, USA

People rummage through open dumps and take electronics apart by hand to scavenge for valuable materials to sell. In the process, they expose themselves to hazardous materials. In China, people burn e-waste in open pits. This contaminates air, soil, and water. Kids play in toxic ash and develop lead poisoning.

DID YOU KNOW?

There's a connection between convenience and recycling. Many people really want to recycle—but only if it's not too difficult. Make it easy for others to pitch in. Take a co-mingled recycling bin, which accepts different types of materials, to practices, games, and activities. Urge others to throw in plastic bottles, cans, and glass instead of lobbing them into trashcans.

All of this points to the need to stop waste before it happens. Maybe you don't always need the latest version of smartphone or gaming console. Before you replace the devices in your house that are still useful, think carefully about where your old ones are going to end up!

Downcycling

Upcycling is using materials to turn them into something new and better. **Downcycling** is the opposite. Downcycling is turning materials into new items of lesser quality. And although recycling is a loop, not all materials can go around and around endlessly, especially paper and plastics. After repeated reprocessing, materials become too broken down to use. Fresh materials must be added to make them usable again.

Conservancy and Stewardship in Action

In 2018, several metro New Orleans, Louisiana, cities and parishes pitched in to recycle and reuse Christmas trees and help restore **wetlands**. Folks dragged evergreen trees to the curbs with their regular trash for collection. When more than 8,000 trees were collected, Louisiana's National Guard airlifted them from the cities to bayous. Adult and student volunteers, including ninth-graders from St. Martin's Episcopal School, loaded the trees onto boats that carried them to marshes. The trees were reused as shoreline fences that prevent wetland soil **erosion**.

National Guard airlifting trees

View this TED Talk to learn about the Ashton Cofer team's hypothesis, failures, and ultimate successes as they tackled the problem of turning Styrofoam into something useful. What will you invent to help the planet?

PS

⌕ TED Talk Ashton Cofer

RUBBISH WARRIORS

Packing peanuts and package cushioning, grab-and-go coffee cups and carry-out containers, swimming boards and ice chests: All are made of Styrofoam. This synthetic, non-renewable material requires more than 500 years to break down.

Granted, it's an inexpensive, efficient packaging material. But in the United States alone, we've produced more than 2 billion pounds of the stuff. Most of it ends up littered across beaches, bobbing in oceans, and jammed into landfills.

Not for long! Meet kid inventor Ashton Cofer. Together with his First Lego League team, Ashton worked to develop a heating treatment that breaks down Styrofoam into components that are useful in other ways. Not only does this keep Styrofoam from littering our land and oceans, it's another way to reuse a resource!

ESSENTIAL QUESTION

How will you challenge yourself to recycle more?

Styrofoam to-go containers
credit: David Gilford (CC BY 2.0)

BAG BREAK DOWN

How long does it take for different types of waste bags to break down? Conduct a three-month study to find out!

❯ **Collect and examine four different kinds of bags:** A large brown grocery bag, a standard plastic trash bag, a biodegradable trash bag, and a compostable trash bag. Start a scientific method worksheet and write descriptions of each in your science journal.

❯ **Cut each bag to a standard size.** Then, take a photo of each bag for comparison later. You'll take a progression of photos over the next three months.

❯ **Use four wooden paint stirrers.** Label each to identify a corresponding bag: "Paper," "Standard Plastic," "Biodegradable," "Compostable."

❯ **In a location where bags can remain undisturbed, dig four 1-foot-deep holes.** Place a different bag in each hole. Cover the holes with soil and place the appropriate paint stirrer marker at each site.

❯ **Predict what will happen over a three-month period.** How will the bags break down? What are observable signs that bags are biodegrading? Will texture and strength change? Which bag will break down first? Why? Jot down your predictions.

❯ **Dig up the buried bags once a month for the next three months.** Wear gloves to examine each bag. How have they changed? Are they the same color? Has their texture or strength changed? Take a photo of each for comparison.

❯ **After three months, dig up the bags a final time.** Compare and contrast your results, and assess your predictions. What conclusions can you draw?

Try This!

They're making a difference! Discover the innovative ideas that middle-school inventors have explored to reduce our waste.

🔎 clever student inventions reduce waste

FUEL FOR THE FIRE

Recycle waste paper to create energy and conserve landfill space. When we recycle, we reduce the necessity of making materials from scratch. We conserve natural resources and reduce the amount of stuff we dump out and throw away.

Caution: Don't use items that contain wax liners, foams, or plastics.

❯ **Gather paper products** such as cereal boxes, grocery bags, paper cups and plates, napkins and paper towels, and flour and sugar bags. Cut them into about 4-inch pieces. Place the pieces in a tub of warm water and thoroughly soak them until they become mushy to the touch. Pour out the water.

❯ **Line a cookie sheet with aluminum foil.** Layer the wet paper squares onto the sheet. Build up layers until they are approximately three-quarters of an inch thick. Press hard with the heel of your hand to compress the layers and squish out the remaining water. Carefully pour out the water.

❯ **Place the cookie sheet in a warm place to dry for at least 24 hours.** Outside in the sun works best.

❯ **When the layers have completely dried, lift the entire piece out of the pan.** Peel away the aluminum foil. Snap or cut off hunks of dried paper to use when you want to build a fire in a fireplace or while camping. They'll burn like wood.

Consider This!

Designed to stand alone or fit into fireplaces, wood pellet stoves use compacted sawdust from processed wood as fuel. During processing, bark gets striped from wood. Then, wood is ground and dried before it's compressed into little pellets about an inch long. How are wood pellets made from recycled wood? Watch a video to observe the process.

🔎 how are wood pellets made

Chapter 8

RETHINK

Rethinking is reconsidering. It's changing your mind about how you deal with an issue. Trash has been with us since our nomadic ancestors scouted for food and water. Garbage is part of our lives and always will be. However, we can rethink the way we deal with the waste in our lives.

First, think about how you produce garbage in the first place. Then, find ways to reduce the amount you throw out. Do this by making wise choices about what you buy. Try to purchase only what you need. Use up everything you have!

You might not see it, but garbage goes somewhere after you toss it out. By the time you doze off tonight, another jam-packed landfill will close. Encourage friends and family to keep trash out of landfills.

ESSENTIAL QUESTION

How can you rethink choices to develop a waste-reduction action plan?

The great news is that you can go about it in lots of sustainable ways. Team up with worms and decomposers to compost organic wastes. Use creativity to repurpose old possessions. Recycle everything you can and buy recycled products.

Choices you make each day really do matter. They make a difference right now and for the future. The earth shares precious resources with you. Making sustainable choices lets you give something back to the planet that keeps you alive.

So, get the word out. Share what you know about garbage and encourage others to help. Every little effort adds up to big changes. As the World Wildlife Fund reminds us, "We need to change the way we live, work, and play. Today."

And don't forget Jack, the student who wrote to the Ocean Conservancy. He put it to us simply: "You guys have to step up . . . ."

Food waste from grocery stores in Sweden

Step up. Make a difference. Change starts with you. You're Earth's future.

As climate change becomes more and more of a problem, people around the world are being affected by more extreme weather events, changing coastlines, and shortages of natural resources, including water. What does your trash have to do with helping people on the other side of the world?

Everything you throw away contributes to the changing environmental balance of the planet. The piece of plastic that falls from your pocket could end up several countries away. While one piece of plastic might not do a huge amount of damage, these individual pieces add up quickly into a major problem. As land and waterways become choked, natural resources get depleted, and carbon and other greenhouse gases filter up into the atmosphere, we all need to take care to limit the damage caused by our daily habits. We need to find new solutions to keep the planet—and our species—healthy.

Picture Perfect

Wilted lettuce. A blemished pear. Brown spots on a banana peel. Zucchini with a wonky shape. Do you turn away "ugly" produce and pitch it in the trash? Ditching imperfect fruits and veggies thwarts efforts to battle poverty, hunger, and climate change. And, when we squander food, we waste money. Some people feel that their food needs to be beautiful for it to appear on their dinner table, but a strange-looking carrot tastes just as good (and is just as good for you!) as a perfectly straight one!

 With your family or classmates, read this article from *The Guardian*. Put your heads together to calculate, rethink, and reduce your own food waste.

🔎 Guardian US food waste

WORDS TO KNOW

gazebo: a type of shelter.

freeganism: a lifestyle that rejects spending money.

Besides, tracking garbage and thinking creatively about different ways to recycle and upcycle is fun! You can come up with incredibly creative art, objects, clothing, and lots of other stuff, all made from—garbage!

RUBBISH WARRIORS

Amelia and Michael Howard shared a dream and were determined to make it come true. The Howards lived on Chicago's South Side, right across the street from a huge vacant lot.

Years earlier, the lot had been a stockyard, where meatpacking companies slaughtered animals. After the stockyards closed in the 1970s, the vacant lot became a hazardous eyesore. Businesses and construction crews ditched contaminated rubble there, creating an open toxic dump. People were exposed to high levels of lead. It wasn't safe for kids to play there.

The Howards rallied their community. Soon all the neighbors shared the Howards' dream: Turn trash into treasure!

Michael Howard rented a bulldozer and with the help of others cleared away 200 tons of waste. Kids piled up bricks and picked up junk. They planted a large community garden. Soon, eggplant, beans, and tomatoes sprouted. Teens built a **gazebo** so visitors could enjoy nature in the city. Volunteers even designed a wetland pond with ducks!

PS Despite mountains of food waste, hunger is a reality. Forty million people in the United States lack nutritional food to thrive. They depend on the Feeding America Network for assistance with food insecurity and hunger relief. **Learn how you can be part of a brighter future.**

🔍 Feeding America food banks

Today, Eden Place Nature Center is an urban oasis for all to enjoy. The center raises chickens and sells organic eggs at the farmers' market. It hosts a popular yearly pumpkin festival. What's next? The possibilities are endless.

Dumpster Gleaning

Cases of bottled water. Sealed boxes of crackers. Bunches of grapes. Whole watermelons. Bags of bagels. All are perfectly edible. And all are tossed in dumpsters outside grocery and convenience stores. Why? Often there's not enough room for older items when new stock arrives. Perhaps an item reached its "sell-by" date, so out it goes. Or a banana, slightly blemished, gets abandoned on the shelves. Dumpster gleaners are ready to swoop in and recover them!

Dumpster gleaning is scouring trash for treasures, often food. Many people who forage in dumpsters time their visits so they recover food a few minutes after it's tossed out. That way, food is straight from the store. Others check with store employees to ask if they can rescue food that's ready to be pitched. They're aware that in many places, dumpster gleaning might not be illegal—but trespassing on private property is.

Freeganism is next-level dumpster gleaning. *Freegan* is a combination of the words *free* and *vegan*. Freegans are devoted to lives of very little spending, limited consumption of resources, and reduced waste. They try not to buy anything or they make extremely minimal purchases. Freegans scavenge retail and business dumpsters to recover discarded goods. They glean from dumpsters at schools and grocery stores. They reclaim reusable items, including furniture, clothing, electronics, personal care items, and food. In the spirit of community and generosity, people get together to share and trade hauls with others.

Many freegans, in protest of massive amounts of food waste, exclusively rely on dumpster gleaning and community gardens for food sources. Some organizations arrange the collection of bread, baked goods, and produce that markets or restaurants are unable to sell or use. Folks prepare recovered food and share meals on the streets.

Food Recovery Hierarchy
www.epa.gov/foodscraps

UNITED STATES ENVIRONMENTAL PROTECTION

Source Reduction
Reduce the volume of surplus food generated

Feed Hungry People
Donate extra food to food banks, soup kitchens and shelters

Feed Animals
Divert food scraps to animal feed

Industrial Uses
Provide waste oils for rendering and fuel conversion and food scraps for digestion to recover energy

Composting
Create a nutrient-rich soil amendment

Landfill/Incineration
Last resort to disposal

During World War II, the nation united in a common goal. Remember that rhyme? "Use it up, wear it out, make it do, or do without." People joined together to cut down their use of resources. Imagine what would happen if everyone pitched in to reduce rubbish and change our throwaway world.

Check out this food waste poster from the EPA. How can you reduce your food waste?

You've met rubbish warriors who are making a difference. Now, become a rubbish warrior yourself! Act! What will you do to help the environment?

ESSENTIAL QUESTION

How can you rethink choices to develop a waste-reduction action plan?

Although she lives in the vast metropolis of New York City, Britta Riley was determined to grow her own food. In her apartment! Through research, testing, and trial-and-error, she developed a vertical **hydroponic** system. Even better? It uses discarded plastic water bottles. **View Britta Riley's TED Talk to check out her system.** How does it inspire you to rethink?

PS

🔎 TED Talk Britta Riley

WINDOWSILL HERB GARDEN

Growing your own food is a fantastic way to conserve energy and resources. For one thing, you won't need fossil fuels for transportation. And no packaging is involved. In this project, grow what you need and eat what you grow with your own indoor herb garden!

Hint: Notice when your plants need to be transplanted into larger pots.

❯ **Choose four kinds of herb seeds, such as basil, oregano, dwarf lavender, and mint.** Use four old spoons and scraps of colorful wallpaper or giftwrap to make decorative plant labels and set them aside.

❯ **Fill each of four 6-inch pots with potting soil or compost.** Sprinkle four individual seeds in the center of each pot, according to the recommended depth. As you plant each type of seed, stick the identifying marker into the soil. Water, but don't drown, each plant. The soil should look wet and feel moist to the touch.

❯ **Place your herb garden on a flat, stable surface in a warm location that receives plenty of sunshine.** Herbs thrive with 6 to 8 hours of sun a day.

❯ **When temperatures drop below freezing, move your garden away from windows.** Keep the pots out of the draft but in the sunlight.

❯ **Depending on the plant, you should see sprouts within three weeks.** Allow the surface soil to become dry to the touch between waterings. When the herbs are fully grown, pinch or snip off bits as needed. Add fragrant basil and oregano to pizza, pasta sauces, and soups. Brew soothing mint tea and dry out lavender for a sweet-smelling potpourri.

Consider This!

Herbs are often used in soaps and lotions. With an adult's permission, do some research on the internet and at the library on making your own soap with your own homegrown herbs!

FRAGRANT HERBAL SHAMPOO

Check out the list of ingredients on your shampoo bottle. Recognize anything? You probably see a lot of long, complicated names such as **sodium laureth sulfate, cinnamidopropyltrimonium chloride,** and **cocamidopropyl betaine.** If you don't like the idea of putting chemicals in your hair, make homemade shampoo using herbs from your indoor garden!

❯ **Crush dried lavender flowers with a rolling pin until you have 4 tablespoons.** With your hands, shred mint leaves into tiny pieces, and measure 4 tablespoons. Place the herbs into a mixing bowl.

❯ **Pour distilled water into a pot and bring it to a vigorous boil.** With help from an adult, remove the pot from the burner and pour 7 ounces of the distilled water over the herbs. Let the herbs soak for 20 to 30 minutes. Check after 20 minutes to see if the scent is strong enough for you. If not, let the herb water sit for 10 more minutes.

❯ **In the meantime, pour 4 tablespoons liquid Castile soap into an empty shampoo container.** When your herbs are ready, strain the herb water so that only liquid remains. Pour it into the shampoo container, and tightly cap it. Shake the shampoo to blend the ingredients. Make sure it's thoroughly cool before use. **Hint:** Do you have light hair? Beware! This recipe could stain your locks with a dark color. Replace lavender flowers and mint leaves with dried chamomile and dried yellow marigolds.

Try This!

Experiment with natural hair conditioners. For example, after you shampoo, massage 2 tablespoons of plain, fresh yogurt into your hair. Wait a few minutes, then rinse.

WORDS TO KNOW

sodium laureth sulfate: a detergent used in shampoos to make it lather up.

cinnamidopropyltrimonium chloride: a sunscreen used in shampoos.

cocamidopropyl betaine: a detergent used in shampoos to make it thicker.

ORGANIZE A NO-WASTE LUNCH

Stop lunch trash! Encourage your school to pitch in—instead of pitching trash out—to make a difference. Challenge everyone to participate in a no-waste lunch.

❯ **Team up with a group of friends.** Speak to your teachers and principal about your plans and arrange a date for the no-waste lunch.

❯ **Make posters and fliers to get the word out.** Include a clever slogan and an eye-catching design. Incorporate information about items that produce waste and those that don't. Publicize the date on your class or school website and during daily announcements. Encourage everyone in your school community to participate.

Investigate organizations dedicated to fighting food loss and waste.

🔎 Foodtank fighting food loss

Try This!

After the no-waste lunch, have a debriefing session. How did things go? What changes will you make for next time? How can you make waste-free lunches a common practice?

Waste	No-Waste
✱ plastic grocery bag or single-serving lunch kit	✱ lunch box, bento box, reusable bag
✱ plastic water bottle, beverage can, juice bag, juice box, mini milk carton, straw	✱ stainless steel water bottle, thermos
✱ paper napkins	✱ cloth napkins
✱ plastic utensils	✱ silverware and chopsticks from home
✱ single-serving bag of pretzels	✱ pretzels in a reusable container
✱ single-serving fruit in a plastic package	✱ apple, banana, orange, peach, or other fruit, cut up in a reusable container
✱ sandwich wrapped in plastic, foil, or wax paper	✱ sandwich packed in a reusable container

algae: a simple organism found in water that is like a plant but without roots, stems, or leaves.

algae bloom: a rapid increase in an aquatic ecosystem's algae population.

archaeologist: a scientist who studies ancient people and their cultures by looking at what they left behind.

artifact: an object made by people from past cultures, including tools, pottery, and jewelry.

bacteria: microorganisms found in soil, water, plants, and animals. Some are harmful, while others are helpful.

biodegradable: able to decay and break down.

biological warfare: using toxins and infectious agents as weapons of war.

bubonic plague: a deadly infectious disease carried by rats and mice that can spread to humans. Also called Black Death.

by-product: an extra and sometimes unexpected or unintended result of an action or process.

capacity: the maximum amount something can hold.

carbon dioxide: a gas formed by the burning of fossil fuels, the rotting of plants and animals, and the breathing out of animals or humans.

castings: rich, digested soil worms leave behind as waste.

catapult: weapon of war used to launch objects over a great distance.

catastrophic: involving or causing large amounts of damage.

cell: a storage space for garbage in a landfill.

chamber pot: a jug or bowl stashed under beds as a personal port-a-potty.

cinnamidopropyltrimonium chloride: a sunscreen used in shampoos.

climate change: a change in long-term weather patterns, which can happen through natural or man-made processes.

closed-loop life cycle: the life cycle for organic material that never comes to an end.

cocamidopropyl betaine: a detergent used in shampoos to make it thicker.

commercial product: a product produced in large quantities by business.

compactor: a machine that tightly packs trash.

compost: decayed food scraps and vegetation that can be put back in the soil. Also, to recycle food scraps and vegetation and put them back in the soil.

compostable: a material that can break down and rot in a compost heap.

compress: to squeeze and squish things to make them smaller.

condensate: a poisonous liquid by-product of gas.

consumerism: a willingness to spend money on goods and services.

contaminant: a poisonous or polluting substance.

contamination: the presence of harmful substances such as contaminants or pollutants in water, soil, or air.

corpse: a dead body.

crops: plants grown for food and other uses.

current: the steady flow of water or air in one direction.

data: information, facts, and numbers.

debris: the scattered pieces of something that has been broken or destroyed.

decay: to rot.

decomposers: bacteria, fungi, and worms that break down wastes and dead plants and animals.

deforestation: the process through which forests are cleared to use land for other purposes.

delirious: a condition of restlessness, confusion, and excitement brought on by a high fever, often with mixed-up speech.

devour: to eat hungrily or greedily.

dioxin: an extremely toxic chemical that can be released from burning some materials.

disposable: made to be thrown away after using once.

downcycle: to recycle materials into something of lesser quality.

dubious: doubtful, uncertain.

ecopod: an ecologically friendly container.

ecosystem: an interdependent community of living and nonliving things and their environment.

edible: safe to eat.

embellishment: decoration, trimming.

emissions: something sent or given off, such as smoke, gas, heat, or light.

engineer: a person who uses science, math, and creativity to design and build things.

entrepreneur: a person who takes a risk to start and operate a business.

Environmental Protection Agency (EPA): a department of the U.S. government concerned with the environment and its impact on human health.

environment: everything in nature, living and nonliving, including animals, plants, rocks, soil, and water.

epidemic: a disease that hits large groups at the same time and spreads quickly.

erosion: the gradual wearing away of rock or soil by water and wind.

e-waste: discarded electronics.

excavate: to dig out a site and its artifacts for study.

exhaust: to use up.

feasibility: achievability.

feces: poop.

festering: rotting.

flammable: something that burns very easily.

food chain: a community of animals and plants where each is eaten by another higher up in the chain.

fossil fuel: a natural fuel that formed long ago from the remains of living organisms. Oil, natural gas, and coal are fossil fuels.

freeganism: a lifestyle that rejects spending money.

fungi: mold, mildew, rust, and mushrooms. Plural of fungus.

garbologist: an archaeologist who studies garbage.

gazebo: a type of shelter.

gizzards: muscular organs in the digestive track.

greenhouse gas: a gas that traps heat in the earth's atmosphere and contributes to the greenhouse effect and global warming.

groundwater: underground water supplies.

gyre: a spiral.

hazardous waste: a waste with properties that make it dangerous or capable of having a harmful effect on human health or the environment.

hydroponic: growing plants in liquid, without using soil.

hype: excitement through a hard-sell approach.

incinerator: a large furnace that burns trash.

industrialized: when there is a lot of manufacturing. Products are made by machines in large factories.

Industrial Revolution: the name of the period of time that started in England in the late 1700s when people started using machines to make things in large factories.

infectious: able to spread quickly from one person to others.

ingenuity: the ability to solve difficult problems creatively.

ingest: to swallow.

innovative: having new ideas about how something can be done.

inorganic: not part of the living world, such as tin and glass.

intact: not damaged.

jettison: to throw something away.

landfill: a huge area of land where trash gets buried.

leachate: a liquid produced in landfills as garbage decays.

linear life cycle: the life cycle for inorganic material that comes to an end when it is thrown away.

livestock: animals raised for food and other products.

manufactured: made by machines.

marine: having to do with the ocean.

maroon: to leave someone or something trapped somewhere that's hard to get to.

medical waste: waste generated at hospitals and doctors' offices, such as needles, bandages, or blood.

methane: a greenhouse gas produced by rotting garbage.

metropolis: a large city.

midden: an ancient garbage heap.

Middle Ages: the period of European history from about the years 350 to 1400.

monitor: to watch, keep track of, or check.

natural resource: a material such as coal, timber, water, or land that is found in nature and is useful to humans.

nomadic: moving from place to place to find food and water.

non-renewable: a natural resource that can be used up, that we can't make more of, such as oil.

nutrients: substances in food and soil that living things need to live and grow.

obsolescence: uselessness.

organic: something that is or was living, such as wood, paper, grass, and insects.

pesticide: a chemical used to kill pests such as rodents or insects.

pollute: to make dirty or unclean with chemicals or other waste.

pomander: ball or perforated container that holds scented materials.

possessions: things you own.

precycling: buying less and creating less waste.

preventive: stopping something before it happens.

processed food: food that has added ingredients to make it look nicer, taste better, last longer, or cost less.

propel: to drive or move forward.

putrid: decaying and smelling bad.

ration: to limit the amount of something to be used each week or month.

recycle: shredding, squashing, pulping, or melting items to use the materials to create new products.

reduce: to use less of something.

refinery: factory where petroleum is separated into different oil types.

renewable: something that can be replaced after we use it.

reprocess: to break down, treat, and prepare to recover materials to use again.

repurpose: to change something and use it for a new purpose.

resource: things found in nature, such as wood or gold, that people can use.

resourceful: able to think of creative solutions to problems.

rethink: to reconsider—to think about something again and change your mind about it.

reuse: instead of tossing out an item, using it again or for a new or creative purpose.

runoff: produced when water picks up wastes as it flows over the surface of the ground. Runoff can pollute streams, lakes, rivers, and oceans.

salvaged: recovered parts or materials that are recycled or reused.

sanitation: conditions relating to public health and cleanliness.

sanitation worker: a person hired to collect and dispose of garbage.

scavenge: to find usable bits and parts from discarded stuff.

sewage: waste from buildings, carried away through sewers.

sewer: a drain for wastewater.

slaughterhouse: a place where animals are killed for food.

slops: a mushy mixture of kitchen scraps and liquid fed to pigs.

sodium laureth sulfate: a detergent used in shampoos to make it lather up.

sorbent: a material that can absorb a liquid or semi-liquid.

source reduction: decreasing the quantity of waste, especially in packaging, so there is less to dispose of.

statistics: numbers that show facts about a subject.

suburb: where people live near a city.

sustainability: living in a way that uses resources wisely, so they don't run out.

technology: the tools, methods, and systems used to solve a problem or do work.

tells: artificial mounds that humans built with garbage.

thrift: using money carefully.

tine: a point.

toxic: poisonous.

toxin: a poisonous or harmful substance.

upcycle: to remake old products into something more environmentally friendly, and often of better quality and value.

vermicomposting: using worms in compost to break down and recycle food wastes.

vermin: small animals or insects that are pests, such as cockroaches or mice.

victory garden: a garden planted by Americans during World War II. About 2 million victory gardens produced 40 percent of the food grown in the United States during the war.

wake: a trail of something left behind.

waste: material that is not wanted.

waste stream: the flow of household and industrial garbage that gets hauled away, recycled, incinerated, or disposed of in landfills.

wastewater: dirty water that has been used by people in their homes, in factories, and in other businesses.

wetlands: low areas filled with water, such as a marsh or swamp.

yellow fever: a disease caused by a virus spread through mosquito bites.

Metric Conversions

Use this chart to find the metric equivalents to the English measurements in this book. If you need to know a half measurement, divide by two. If you need to know twice the measurement, multiply by two. How do you find a quarter measurement? How do you find three times the measurement?

English	Metric
1 inch	2.5 centimeters
1 foot	30.5 centimeters
1 yard	0.9 meter
1 mile	1.6 kilometers
1 pound	0.5 kilogram
1 teaspoon	5 milliliters
1 tablespoon	15 milliliters
1 cup	237 milliliters

RESOURCES

MUSEUMS

Explore the Eco Challenge exhibit at the Discovery Science Foundation Cube in Santa Ana, California: *oc.discoverycube.org/exhibits/eco-challenge*

How about a virtual tour of the astonishing Rubbish Collection at London's Science Museum?: *blog.sciencemuseum.org.uk/tag/the-rubbish-collection*

VIDEOS

Watch this video for a quick overview of the history of garbage collectors from the Black Plague to the present: *youtube.com/watch?v=UtqR_mDPDkY*

Get behind the wheel of the massive TANA E320eco landfill compactor: youtube.com/watch?v=bBLOCTrPZ1c

NASA created an amazing scientific visualization to illustrate the ways ocean garbage patches have developed: youtube.com/watch?v=mMG1SdeYLFE

Conveyer belts, scanners, machines! Experience mechanisms that daily move 800 tons of recyclables through Brooklyn's Sim Municipal recycling plant: youtube.com/watch?v=nUrBBBs7yzQ

Author, gleaner, and food waste warrior Tristram Stuart presents a talk on *The Beauty of Ugly Food*: video.nationalgeographic.com/video/00000148-bd38-d00e-adef-ffbc74fb0000

ARTICLES AND WEBSITES

Here's a handy visual to illustrate Ocean Plastic by the Numbers: kids.nationalgeographic.com/explore/nature/kids-vs-plastic/ocean-plastic-by-the-numbers

There's more! Enjoy incredible photographs from the Science Museum's Rubbish Collection: *theguardian.com/culture-professionals-network/gallery/2014/jul/30/waste-not-science-museum-rubbish-collection-in-pictures*

What artifacts did archaeologists dig up in President George Washington's trash heaps?: slate.com/human-interest/2013/09/george-washington-what-archaeologists-found-in-his-trash-heap-at-mt-vernon.html

Scientists at the University of Portsmouth in England accidentally created a plastic-gobbling enzyme: *independent.co.uk/news/science/plastic-eating-enzyme-pollution-solution-waste-bottles-bacteria-portsmouth-a8307371.html*

Trash to treasure! Landfill parks have sprung up in communities around the world: inhabitat.com/8-incredible-parks-created-from-landfills

RESOURCES

QR CODE GLOSSARY

page 6: *youtube.com/watch?v=eym10GGidQU*

page 11: *youtube.com/watch?time_continue=43&v=LZ71svh1RVo*

page 13: *washingtonpost.com/news/energy-environment/wp/2018/03/22/ plastic-within-the-great-pacific-garbage-patch-is-increasing-exponentially- scientists-find/?noredirect=on&utm_term=.ad624dc3625b*

page 14: *youtube.com/watch?v=ju_2NuK5O-E*

page 16: *nationalgeographic.com/environment/planetorplastic*

page 18: *nces.ed.gov/nceskids/createagraph*

page 29: *www.smithsonianmag.com/videos/category/ science/climate-change-101-with-bill-nye-the-science*

page 30: *youtube.com/watch?v=Q6eBJjdca14*

page 31: *smithsonianmag.com/science-nature/ from-gunpowder-to-teeth-whitener-the-science-behind-historic-uses-of-urine-442390*

page 32: *streetsofsalem.com/2016/12/11/pomanders-and-the-plague*

page 37: *saveonenergy.com/land-of-waste*

page 39: *youtube.com/watch?v=ImppGpYuYh4*

page 42: *youtube.com/watch?v=z7EEC3ctQro*

page 43: *noaa.gov/media-release/gulf-of-mexico-dead-zone-is-largest-ever-measured*

page 47: *youtube.com/watch?v=dA4x7RIj3-U*

page 48: *vimeo.com/33313404*

page 52: *archive.nytimes.com/www.nytimes.com/ interactive/2010/04/28/us/20100428-spill-map.html*

page 53: *theatlantic.com/technology/archive/2018/01/the-oil-spill-that-wasnt/550820*

page 58: *climate.nasa.gov/blog/2357*

page 68: *marketplace.org/2013/03/12/life/big-book/ processed-foods-make-70-percent-us-diet*

page 73: *youngvoicesfortheplanet.com/youth-climate-videos/the-last-straw*

page 80: *hyperallergic.com/368152/nyc-trash-is-a-museum-of-treasure*

page 84: *hugitforward.org*

page 87: *dmachoice.org*

RESOURCES

ESSENTIAL QUESTIONS

Introduction: Why does it matter where our garbage goes after we throw it out?

Chapter 1: Do you produce more inorganic or organic waste?

Chapter 2: How has garbage dumping changed throughout history?

Chapter 3: What role do landfills play in solid-waste management?

Chapter 4: How does hazardous waste cause problems in landfills and the environment?

Chapter 5: How will you precycle and reduce to limit what you dump into the waste stream?

Chapter 6: How can you use creativity and ingenuity to reuse items?

Chapter 7: How will you challenge yourself to recycle more?

Chapter 8: How can you rethink choices to develop a waste-reduction action plan?

INDEX